PREFACE

What a way to celebrate the Fortieth Anniversary of the founding of Sun City Center and the Thirtieth of Kings Point! Tony Shuen had the inspiration to ask for recollections from residents to mirror the reflection of a town "too busy to retire."

He wanted to make a compilation of articles in the form of a book to be called Celebrating Sun City Center. He formed a partnership to achieve this goal consisting of Dr. Phil Lange, John Bowker, Bob Wicklund and Tricia Smith. Bob Wicklund became the project manager. The rest of us read his job description as " HELP!" Bob was up for any job concerning this publication and has been invaluable to all of us. Phil Lange, John Bowker and Tricia Smith form the Editorial Board, choosing and arranging the submissions. Don Pagano is our computer consultant and has been responsible for creating the computer - generated documents. His technical expertise with digital images of both photographs and documents resulted in their enhancement to meet the high standards of the publisher. Bette Mederich is chief assistant to Tony and is the Treasurer. Bill Hoskins helped us as an expert typist and, Linda Bowker as a proof-reader.

Seated: l. to r. Phil Lange, Tricia Smith, Bob Wicklund Standing: Tony Shuen, Bette Mederich, Bill Hoskins, Linda Bowker, John Bowker, and Don Pagano

In some four or five articles in the local newspapers we requested submissions from residents telling their impressions of Sun City Center. Some of those who replied drew upon a hoard of many years' memories and some who have recently moved here look at Sun City Center with a newcomer's appreciation. We have the reflections of some who have had a great impact on the community like Dr. Robert Gingery and Dr. Dallas Tuthill. Beside the residents, there are those who work with us in the community or who report on our doings. Al Hoffman, the developer and CEO of the WCI Corporation, Penny Fletcher of the Sun Newspaper and Brenda Knowles of the Observer have kindly sent their thoughts about us.

A very popular topic was "Why I came to Sun City Center." Several stories tell about finding a new career here after retiring. Enthusiastic members give an insight into the sports, clubs and other activities. The functions of the organizations which form the backbone of our care and security, like the Emergency Squad, the Security Patrol, Samaritan Services and the Community Foundation of Greater Sun City Center, are also explained.

Part II of the book is totally made up of photographs of Greater Sun City Center. Most of the photos were taken by Tony Shuen over an extended period of time with some assistance from Bob Wicklund. Tony's goal was to capture the essence of the activities and life-style of Sun City Center in colored photos, from its volunteer Association management to its self-managed clubs, sports and support services, its many churches and temple, as well as its stellar maintenance staff.

The result of the meld of Part I and Part II is a kaleidoscopic view of our wonderful town and its residents. Our hope is that Celebrating Sun City Center will be a living legacy.

Tricia Smith

Tricia Smith
Editor In Chief

PAGE NO.

VOLUNTEERISM – MAKING A DIFFERENCE

POETIC CONTRIBUTIONS

ON THE LIGHT SIDE

SPORTS, ACTIVITIES AND CLUBS

VITAL ORGANIZATIONS

OTHER MAJOR ORGANIZATIONS

VIGNETTES

NEW OUTLOOKS

History of Greater Sun City Center

John Bowker

It all started with the worst traffic jam this part of Florida had ever experienced. New Year's Weekend, 1962. Press reports indicate that over 40,000 of the curious ventured over a two-lane, shell-gravel road (State Road 674 even in those days) to see what this Del Webb experiment in retirement living really meant.

A 13,000 acre cow pasture was purchased next to the proposed path of a new interstate highway (now I-75). Ground breaking took place on May 10, 1961 and, amazingly, the Grand Opening was on January 1, 1962. By then, model homes with landscaping, paved streets leading to them, an operating hotel with fine restaurant, a shopping plaza including at least a grocery supermarket, a general store, and a functioning post office were all ready for the first residents. There was a problem about the name of the community; Webb wanted "Sun City" but another community just south of Ruskin held the name and no amount of persuasion would convince the residents there to change to something else. In concert with the postal authorities, Sun City Center was finally adopted. The Grand Opening occurred right on schedule.

Del Webb continued to develop Sun City Center for a decade but then, after suffering a number of set-backs, largely due to the economy, he sold the remaining development to a local firm headed by Jim Walter and Gerry Gould, operating under the name "W-G." New house styles appeared, the hotel that had burned to the ground a year earlier was rebuilt and, once again, Sun City Center was on the road to success. Mortgage notes were taken with the First National Bank of Chicago (FNBC), the entire southwest portion of the property was sold to a condominium developer from the east coast called "Kings Point", and financing appeared to be secure. But spiraling interest rates and a gasoline shortage cut off any chance W-G had of making a go of it. In fact, the Kings Point developer had also taken a note with the FNBC and there came a time that the bank was forced to call in the notes and take over development of both communities. Ever since then, the two communities have been developed by a common builder; there have been four since W-G.

In 1982 a new facility appeared here, Trinity Lake Towers -- later shortened to Lake Towers. The new high-rise apartment complex offered a growing senior population a place right in town to be comfortable and relieved of day-to-day maintenance of their home. It wasn't long before an assisted living wing was added to "The Towers."

A hospital was built that same year and doctors' offices multiplied. Churches began to appear -- the first was the United Community Church. Freedom Plaza complex and its multi-service functions came a decade later followed shortly by the CourtYards and then Aston Gardens.

The Historical Society of Greater Sun City Center serves as a collection point for early artifacts of the community. Your attention and interest are invited to explore the early concepts, goals, development and the people who have volunteered to make these communities what they are today.

PART ONE

A Collection of Articles Written
and
Contributed
by
The Residents
Of
Greater Sun City Center

There's Something Special About Sun City Center

Al Hoffman Jr.

When I look back upon some of the most important milestones of my business career, one that will always stand out is the purchase of the remaining land and amenities at Sun City Center on December 17, 1987. I was already familiar with the area through my involvement with nearby Walden Lake and instinctively knew that the retirement industry in Florida had only one place to go and that was UP!

In retrospect, my instincts were definitely on target. Through the decade of the 1990's more than 1.2 million people age 50 and older moved to Florida from other states, and the active adult community business became one of the fastest growing segments of the home-building industry. Today, I can look back fondly on my experiences at Sun City Center and see how those experiences helped WCI Communities become one of America's largest home-building companies.

Despite the odds, we completed the acquisition and immediately began the process of revitalizing the community. One of our first projects was the beautification of Highway 674. That project, completed through a public/private partnership between the state and Florida Design Communities, as we were known then, allowed some aspiring business executives - Jerry Starkey, Charlie Brasington and Gary Nelson - to get a good taste of the community development business. I'm proud that, 15 years later, these men are still with me - Jerry as President of WCI Communities, Charlie as President of our West Central Home-building Division that manages our operations at Sun City Center, and Gary as Vice President of Land Development.

While the physical facilities are the mechanisms that help the residents of Sun City Center lead vital, active and fulfilling lives, the heart and soul of the community truly reside in the people. The interactions I have had with the residents of Sun City Center are by far the most enduring memories I have of my long relationship with the community.

The intellectual wealth that resides in Sun City Center is, without a doubt, its most valuable attribute. As I look back upon the many, many meetings I have had with different groups and individuals, I have always been impressed with their grasp of the facts and their understanding of the issues. I came to learn that whatever the issue, the people at the table had studied it deeper and further and, as such, were well prepared for a discussion.

The generosity and caring nature of Sun City Center residents is another quality that is sometimes shadowed by the golf, swimming, craft classes and other recreational pursuits that keep residents so busy.

However, my observations and experiences have turned me into a raving fan when it comes to the topic of volunteerism at Sun City Center. Our research has shown that literally thousands of residents donate hundreds of thousands of hours to improving the quality of life in Sun City Center and its neighboring communities.

I sometimes wonder if future generations of Americans will embody the same type of altruism that can be found today in Sun City Center. President George H.W. Bush coined the phrase "a thousand points of light" and I can think of no better way to acknowledge the contributions that so many people have made to their community over the years. This is what has made Sun City Center such a special place.

No one can spend a decade in a place like Sun City Center and not be changed by the experience. During the last 15 years, I have watched the careers of employees' blossom at Sun City Center. I have watched the community grow, housing styles change and recreational facilities evolve along with the changing needs of the marketplace. I have met a great many people and been impressed time and again with their thoughtfulness, respect, wisdom and determination - attributes that have become all too uncommon today.

There's definitely something special about Sun City Center. It holds a special place in my heart, and it's my sincere hope that the community occupies a special place in the hearts of the people of Sun City Center too.

The Changes I've Seen and Written About

Penny Fletcher

As the editor of the Sun and the South Shore News, I've had the unique opportunity to interview hundreds of our residents. My coverage area extends from Bloomingdale Avenue in Riverview to the Manatee County line.

Together, the two newspapers cover the area that's now known as South Shore. That name's new. For a long time, the same area was called East Bay. Then, following an unsuccessful secession effort in 1988, residents began to call it "South County," which two groups of secessionists - "Write to Secede" and "Citizens for a New County" - had suggested as the new county's name.

A lot of things have changed in South Shore since I started writing about it. One of the biggest is the way Sun City Center is perceived by those in the surrounding towns.

When I first started at the Sun in 1988 most Sun City Center residents weren't involved with the rest of South Shore. On the whole, they had little to do with their neighbors.

Sun City Center then was only half the size it is today. Golf carts were not legal on the street, although many residents drove them there. And the Community Association was still perfecting the fine points of the 1984 Agreement, a legal document which governs the relationship between the community and its developer.

On the whole, the community was very adversarial. Many people were engaged in neighborhood fights and courtroom duels. Golfers were protesting policies of the developer with signs in the streets. Two national golf magazines set reporters to cover the picketing, which was in response to the developer's policy of offering golf to prospective homebuyers. Area residents said they were being crowded off the courses.

Throughout the '80s, residents feared running for Community Association board seats because they were often publicly ridiculed. Some were even ousted.

Thanks to good leadership, this scenario has changed dramatically.

Where once volunteerism was limited to the confines of the Sun City Center community, now help was being offered to residents of Ruskin, Wimauma and other neighboring communities through programs that aided the poor, helped schools and students and offered man-hours and money to a plethora of causes.

New relationships were forged within Sun City Center too. Sun City Center and Kings Point - once openly intolerant of each other - began to work together as one. Leaders found there was more strength in a community united than when fragmented groups each insisted on getting their own way.

Sun City Center's governing entities have run the gamut from isolationism to talk of incorporation and the formation of a city government. Its people have won the respect and attention of county and state officials, both because of their voting strength and dedication to making their part of the world a better place.

The town that was started not as a community but as a "social experiment" has changed greatly over the years. As the editor of its newspaper, and the newspaper for towns around it, my position has been rewarding. It used to be that residents of other areas of South Shore looked at most of Sun City Center as the entity that protested growth and development. To them, that meant a lack of homes and jobs. I used to say my two readerships were diametrically opposed. They aren't anymore. The people in both areas seem to look at each other with more respect. The walls are coming down. Coalitions have been formed that benefit all residents. Young and old and rich and poor from all walks of life are coming together.

Over the years, Sun City Center residents taught others to monitor area development and to protect their resources. Many environmental projects have succeeded because of this. On the other hand, Sun City Center residents have learned they need the goods and services new jobs and businesses in the towns around them will bring.

It has been quite an experience to write about the area for the past 16 years. It's been even a better experience to have lived in it.

And The Beat Goes On

Brenda Knowles

My first contact with Sun City Center was a chance encounter. It was the summer of 1969 when my fiance and I were looking for a house to rent in the Ruskin area. After a half-a-day spent wandering the roads of a budding Brandon and a rural Ruskin, we found ourselves on S.R. 674 in the midst of a delightful subdivision, Sun City Center.

We were immediately impressed with the wide streets, sidewalks and cozy homes with outside lanterns and matching mailboxes. We had found our first home together as husband and wife, or so we thought. Delightful anticipation quickly turned to utter disappointment when we were informed of the age requirements. We would have to wait 34 years to become members of the community.

Not wishing to give up on our retirement village, I was a frequent visitor at the model home center. I remember walking through the developer's reception area, today occupied by the World Center Bank and Winn Dixie, into the fully furnished model homes similar to today's new Welcome Center by the I-75. They were exquisitely attired and a newlywed's dream ... especially the driftwood dining table that beckoned to me each time I visited.

In the mid-70s we saw many movies at the movie theatre located in the Sun City Center Plaza. When my son was 5 years old, he and his father saw "Star Wars" together for the first time.

It wasn't until I started working for the Observer News in 1988 that I really became acquainted with the residents of Sun City Center. That was just about the time the community was beginning to reach out to the other communities of Ruskin, Apollo Beach, Wimauma and Riverview. Up until that time Sun City Center was pretty much closed to the rest of the county. One of the more memorable events that took place in the retirement community was when the developer wanted to build timeshare units within the boundaries of Sun City Center. The residents organizational skills surfaced and soon travelers on S.R. 674 were greeted with protest lines and placards reminiscent of the 60s.

Key words associated with the residents are: volunteerism, generosity and active-lifestyle. Residents of the community are generous with not only their time but also their money. All of the local schools have benefited from the thousands of hours Sun City Center residents have spent in the classroom helping young students with reading, math and social skills.

Each year, East Bay High School and Riverview High School benefit from the generosity of Sun City Center organizations in the form of scholarships. They also help the young juveniles at the correctional institution in Balm.

Active is such a small word to describe the lifestyle of an average resident of Sun City Center. With over 100 clubs and organizations, not counting the Security Patrol, Emergency Squad, the library or Samaritan Services, residents are continually busy. Over the years I have had the pleasure of working with a variety of Sun City Center's finest: Cam Waldeck, Phil Lange, Lee DiAngelo, Janet Wilson, Pat Leahy, Mable Godfrey, Tod McGinley, Renee Deutel, Len Perry, John Smucker, Dolores Berens, John Bowker, Selma Pellegrino, Jim Cooper, Bo Heininger and Dallas Tuthill just to name a few.

As I conclude my trip down memory lane, I am amazed that the year is 2002 and it's 34 years later. The wait is over. Look out, Sun City Center, here comes another "Baby Boomer."

Keep The Spirit

Mary Jane Tovey

Once upon a time in the "sixties something" one man had a vision. "Let's build a new kind of village where middle-class Americans can retire with dignity." After all, they have worked for years to run our companies, build our communities, fight our wars, etc., etc. Wouldn't it be nice for them to have a place to live where they would have congenial neighbors who shared common life experience? They should have homes that are easy to care for so they have time and energy to pursue some of the "fun hobbies" they did not have time to enjoy while they were so busy building America and raising their families.

"Those homes should not cost their entire life savings either! They will need spaces to build churches for all faiths so they can find spiritual strength. They will need pleasant meeting rooms where they can gather together for hobbies and games. if they have lots of people around them, they will keep their minds active and have a better quality of life in their retirement. That might even save some money for the Government in the long run! Imagine a whole town of older folks taking care of themselves!!!"

Impossible? Sun City Center developed from just such a vision, the vision of a dreamer and entrepreneur named Del Webb.

I am one of the lucky people who found a home here. No, the Community Association did not buy my house and no, the Corporation does not directly provide for my mental or physical health care, but it certainly does provide a climate conducive to both! I have a wonderful fitness center, swimming pools, and more sports facilities than I could ever possibly use to help me keep physically fit. I can safely walk on level sidewalks all year round and enjoy the beauty of well-kept gardens. I can walk to the library or game rooms for some mental stimulation. I can relax and feel secure knowing that my very own friends and neighbors will be there for me in any emergency through the Emergency Squad, the Security Patrol and Samaritan Services. Without the support provided for all of us by the Community Association, where would those services ever find enough volunteers? I can easily meet new friends because I am constantly in touch with people my age who share my many interests. I'm proud of the fact that teams of social scientists from England and Japan have recently toured our fine village to learn how are able to provide all this.

And these grand facilities did not just happen. They were carefully planned to facilitate the lifestyle we now enjoy. They depend on the thousands of volunteer members who continue to maintain and improve them. The clubs and organizations are the engines that keep the town running. The Community Association is the caretaker. The Members are the heart and soul, and volunteerism is the Spirit of Sun City Center.

My husband, Lou, and I thank God for leading us here in 1988. I am grateful for having an opportunity to serve on the Board of Directors. We joined a variety of the many clubs and enjoyed everyone we tried. We have received much satisfaction from our volunteer efforts with the C.A. Board, Security Patrol and Samaritan Services. We have learned new skills, developed new hobbies and made many wonderful friends. I found it inspiring to meet alert, active folks still enjoying life in their 90's. We found you can be as busy as you choose, or retreat and meditate if you prefer.

We look forward to many more experiences in Sun City Center. For now we can only say, "Thanks, Sun City Center! Keep the Spirit!"

A Love Affair with a Town

Edward T. Smith

How could a person, or a couple, become enamored with a physical entity -- like a collection of homes and streets and facilities and people – to the point of feeling "in love" with it? Such seems sorta silly, in a way, and when the time comes to try and locate the ideal place to retire and spend the balance of one's life, are we searching for that place that is so ideal that one can "fall in love with it"?

Well, such a search is certainly not easy. A community where one can find peace and quiet, where one could awaken every morning and have available an almost unbelievable variety of interesting and challenging indoor and outdoor pursuits; where weather is absolutely ideal ninety percent of the time, where neighbors are congenial, and costs are reasonable. Does such a place exist?

My wife, Linda, and I had just about reached that point of starting the search back in 1980, and owning part of a fast aircraft allowed us to investigate a variety of retirement communities in several southern states in a short period. One of them happened to be Sun City Center which, by pure accident caught our attention in an advertisement noticed only by the casual turn of a page in a magazine. Had we ignored that magazine, our ensuing life would have been totally different from what has happened.

The ad we found prompted a trip to Sun City Center in 1981 from our home in a small town 1,000 miles to the north of Florida, and we succumbed to a so called "Week of Sun Days" promotion by the developer. I must admit we were more than mildly impressed by what we saw. Beautiful, perfectly kept homes, immaculate yards and sidewalks on both sides of every street, golf courses and tennis courts, indoor and outdoor swimming pools, meeting rooms and more than 100 activity clubs. The community-owned-and-operated Security Patrol and Emergency Squad, local hospital, shopping centers and a surrounding rural atmosphere extending 20 miles from city congestion.

After several trips here I suppose we must admit that we truly did "fall in love" with the place. It seemed to us to be the ideal retirement town. We bought a lot, designed what was to be our "ideal home", drew the plans in detail, negotiated with the developer and, after our first 18 years as residents, can't think of a thing we'd change!

Our retirement home was completed in the last week of December 1984 and the moving van unloaded our belongings a few days before Christmas. By Christmas Day, of course, nothing was set up suitably for cooking and so, in the midst of unloading and unpacking, we had no choice at noon but to visit one of the local fast-food joints – our first Christmas dinner in Sun City Center consisted of a cold sandwich and a Coke. Did we mind? Not in the least. We were, after all, moving into our final home on earth and were literally so excited that consumption of the cold sandwich was mixed with laughter over the situation – as though we were a couple of couldn't-care-less kids.

Although changing somewhat in character as time passes, some basic precepts remain the same. We continue as a "volunteer community." One of our neighbors came by after we'd been here no more than a week and asked if I would be willing to serve on the local residents' Security Patrol that operates marked patrol cars around the whole town and around the clock. I volunteered on the spot and spent the next two years driving on a regular schedule, watching for any irregularities throughout the community. Since that time, I have also served six years on the Community Association's Board of Directors – the organization that manages the recreational facilities on behalf of the residents. I have also served as President of the Sun City Center Tennis Association during which, in 1991, I produced all the plans and specifications for our current tennis facilities consisting of ten soft-surface courts having the finest playing surfaces available anywhere in the world.

Florida is known for the hurricanes that sometimes pass through parts of the state between May and November of each year. However, a hurricane has *never* passed through Sun City Center -- and shall we all now line up and knock on wood??

What's Not to Like?

by Paul Wheat

A quickly-compiled list of reasons why my wife Jean and I chose to live in Sun City Center easily exceeded a couple of dozen. After eight years, those reasons always make us look forward to returning here after our travels. The first attraction for us, as for most people, I suspect, is that we are in an ideal location as far as climate and travel are concerned. It is a short drive to visit many tourist attractions, entertainment, cultural activities, good restaurants, and airports. We have quick access to I-75 and the rest of the interstate highway system, and family and friends from the U.S. and Europe find it easy (maybe sometimes too easy) to get to us.

Our cost of living is reasonable. There is a wide variety of shopping areas nearby, and a number of medical, financial and religious organizations. And where else can these facilities be reached by golf cart?

Having traveled and lived in many neighborhoods, we now live in the best neighborhood ever. We know our neighbors, we communicate and socialize with them, and we look out for and help each other. This certainly is a key factor in our quick dismissal of any thought of re-location.

While we were deciding where to retire, I carefully read the material provided to us in a package by the sales agent. The availability of many services such as The Good Samaritans, Guardianship Foundation, and the United Community Church College really impressed us. Various veterans organizations and support groups were available (and subsequently have been expanded, and new ones organized.) Of particular interest were the Emergency Squad and the Security Patrol. Later on I realized the important roles played in the Sun City Center lifestyle by such as the Men's Club, Woman's Club, SCC Ride, the Community Foundation of Greater Sun City Center, and numerous others.

Without doubt there is no other community with the breadth of activities and amenities available to residents. It didn't take long after our arrival before I was involved in pitching horseshoes, taking golf lessons and trying to imitate a golfer, neighborhood activities, participating in several veterans and social organizations, and an almost full-time job on the Community Association Board of Directors. Soon I was following a schedule which almost demanded I take a refresher course in "time management."

It soon became apparent to us that the cost of enjoying all these activities and amenities is considerably lower than most other communities, largely resulting from the pervasive spirit of "volunteerism." Volunteers make our "physical plant" much less expensive to operate. Volunteers extend the impact and usefulness of many funded organizations and activities. Volunteers extend the influence of our community to surrounding communities, and affect the interaction of SCC with the county and state. In short, volunteers make the attractive Sun City Center "lifestyle" affordable and unique.

SCC—A Miracle for Me

by Susie Van Nostrand

Coming to Sun City Center was a true miracle for me.

I came to Sun City Center when I married my wonderful husband Al VanNostrand. We both had computers and met in a chat room for "Over 50s." We saw each other off and on for a couple of years, and finally tied the knot on Aurust 1, 1998. We were married in SCC at the United Community Church on Pebble Beach Blvd.

After the beautiful ceremony and honeymoon, we moved into my brand new husband's home on Danbury Drive. We later moved to another home on Flamingo Drive. How we loved that house! But as things happen, we moved back to my home town in Ohio, and are taking care of my mentally handicapped son.

One day we hope to come back. I cannot tell you how wonderful we always felt in Sun City Center. The people were just terrific! My husband, Al, happily worked on the SCC Emergency Squad for 5 years until he had to give it up for medical reasons.

We loved to zip around town on our golf cart, going up and down the different roads, looking at the many attractive homes. The area is so clean, friendly and nice. One of our favorite places, where we made several friends, was the garden place where Tillers and Toilers grow their plants and vegetables.

One of my best friends was the alligator that hung out in front of Kings Point. I knew nothing about alligators, and was just sure he would want to become my friend. Well, the day I tried to walk closer to see him and he rose up and hissed, I knew the friendship was over.

I'd Recommend SCC's Lifestyle to Anyone

by Walt Cawein

The answer to the question, "Why did you move to Sun City Center?" becomes easier the longer I live in Sun City Center. Obviously, when one considers a move to a new geographic area one looks for an environment with nice weather, and a community that meets your social, emotional, spiritual and financial needs. Of all the communities we visited prior to moving to Sun City Center, there is no doubt in my mind that Sun City Center offers the best overall lifestyle and quality of life for the money.

Initially, I was impressed with the appearance of the community, including the landscaping along Highway 674, the very neat lawns and homes throughout our community, all of the activities and clubs available to members, and the developer who treated us very professionally, and delivered us a very nice home at a very moderate price.

What was not so apparent at the beginning is the unique brand of volunteerism that has become the hallmark of our lifestyle. Very quickly I learned that SCC is not a retirement community as advertised, but a community of doers, and doers, and doers—most of them spending their valuable time enriching the lives of others. It has been my pleasure to have been able to serve the community as a member of the Community Association Board of Directors.

As a retiree of the military, and the federal government, I wanted to locate near a military base, preferably an Air Force Base, and nearby MacDill AFB fulfilled that desire. Additionally, we wanted to be located near professional sports, theatres, restaurants, and medical facilities. Not only are many of these amenities located in our own backyard, but from Sun City Center one can go north or south on easily-accessed Interstate 75 to Brandon, Tampa, Bradenton and/or Sarasota for an unlimited supply of these activities and events.

I am thankful we made the decision to move to Sun City Center. I have met some wonderful people who I hope will continue to be my friends for the rest of my life. God bless Sun City Center and those who make it a wonderful place to live.

I would recommend Sun City Center's lifestyle to anyone.

WHAT ARE WE ALL ABOUT? VOLUNTEERISM!
by Tricia Smith

The strong and enduring thread that spins its way throughout the 40 years of existence of Sun City Center is the mighty force of volunteerism. The Emergency Squad and the Security Patrol are most in evidence, protecting our health and the safety of our homes.. Men's Club - sponsored Lifeline Medical Alert adds another dimension to health care., informing authorities of a patient's need for emergency help. The Men's Club gave the community a Parkinson's Support Group as well as Man to Man, the Prostate Cancer support group.

The Guardianship Foundation offers a unique gift to residents who are no longer able to handle their own financial obligations. The Good Samaritans see to it that residents who can no longer drive are transported to medical appointments in Tampa and beyond if need be. They have many caring programs for the elderly

The latest addition to the welfare and comfort of residents in 2002 is SCC Ride. These volunteer drivers take housebound or disabled residents where ever they need to go for appointments in Sun City Center. Monitors at the Fitness Center and the pools do their vigilance taking care that no one gets hurt keeping in shape.

One group of volunteers who are often overlooked are those who perform uncounted hours of service on the Community Association Board. Sometimes they are rewarded by criticism of their efforts instead of appreciation. Most of us feel relief when we go to the polls to vote to allow this group of selfless residents to shoulder the responsibilities of running a community the size and complexity of ours. In this year of celebration we certainly owe a debt of gratitude to the hard working Board, Vice President, Walt Cawein and its outgoing President, Jerry Milton.

Volunteers at the many churches in Sun City Center are responsible for casting sunlight in many lives. The Interfaith Council with representatives from all the local churches sponsors the Nearly New Shop and has given scholarships in the amount of $25,000 every year for some time as well as giving to eight or ten outlying charities, the money earned by this dedicated group under the leadership of Dorothy Apgar.

The Greater Sun City Center Foundation has been responsible for many grants for good causes. Its new president, Sally Hahn, is also dean of the Community Church College, another volunteer activity which gives a lot of satisfaction and stimulation to the residents of Sun City Center with its varied curriculum. Phil Lange's Issues and Ideas on Monday afternoons provide provocative, informative and fun programs for the whole community. He has put on more than 700 enthusiastically received programs without missing one. The community couldn't live without John Bowker's "e-news." In 2002 he published a

History of Sun City Center, Part I which was free to every household. He and Mary Lou Munro have headed the staff of the News of Sun City Center which keeps the community up to date on local happenings. A recent changing of the guard finds Judy Krody and Paul Courter in command.

There are some special groups who have spread their focus to the neighboring community of Wimauma. As a matter of fact Mac Mc Comb mentions that it was seeing the need for a helping hand there that influenced his decision to move to Sun City Center. He offers his services at the Wimauma Elementary School, the Yes Program for troubled boys and many other projects. He is president of WAIA (Wimauma Area Improvement Authority), a program pioneered some years ago by Dr. Robert Gingery to provide low cost housing in Wimauma.

The plight of the Migrant Farmworkers of Wimauma was the subject of a book written by Tony Shuen and Tricia Smith in 2000. We covered the several effective ways of helping the Hispanic population there, offering low cost housing (Newmauma Homes, Homes for Hillsborough, La Estancia); Beth-El Mission's many programs (education for children and adults; legal assistance; regular distribution of food and clothing); the many efforts of RCMA (Redlands Christian Migrant Association); the Mission of Nuestra Senora de Guadalupe which supplies education and care for its many Catholic Wimauma residents

Bethune Park's remarkable success as a recreational facility for small children under the leadership of Carla Miles is one of our studies. A copy of the book is available in the Sun City Center Library, another outstanding entity manned with volunteer participation.

Our first copy was sent to First Lady Laura Bush who champions faith-based education. We felt she would be interested in what was happening in our neighboring community. Her response indicated that we were right. We include it with this manuscript.

Of course all the clubs in Sun City Center have volunteers and even our neighborhoods have diligent helpers. On all sides the feeling within the community is "Enjoy our halcyon years to their fullest by helping others to enjoy theirs."

THE WHITE HOUSE

July 25, 2001

Mrs. Harry L. Smith
Number 105
241 Courtyards Boulevard
Sun City Center, Florida 33573-5780

Dear Ms. Smith:

Thank you for your letter and for sending me the first copy of *Wimauma's Migrant Farmworkers*. Congratulations to you and Dr. Anthony Shuen for combining narrative and photos to tell the story of the Wimauma community and its relationship with Sun City Center.

Because of the efforts of volunteers such as those of Sun City Center, much is accomplished that would otherwise be only imagined. Part of the strength and beauty of our country lies in the selfless spirit of those who see needs and create wonderful ways to fill them. I appreciate your sharing their story with me.

With best wishes,

"A Healthy Outlook"

by Curt & Pat Keeler

On 10 April, 1985, I had a heart attack. What a way to celebrate my birthday! Subsequent to my hospitalization, I immediately purchased a stationary bicycle and rowing machine to supplement my two mile walk every morning. This was my daily therapeutic regimen before going to work each day.

The company I worked for, Eastern Airlines, was going through the turmoil that most companies go through when approaching bankruptcy. My wife, Pat, felt that the upheaval in the airline, coupled with my heart attack a few years earlier, was sufficient grounds to call it quits. It was a sad and stressful time in our lives, so on 31 January, 1987, I retired from my grand old company.

We had already had our land purchased and were prepared to move to our future retirement home in Sarasota, Florida. We excitedly looked forward to living in our new location. We even selected the exact location for continued use of my stationary bike and rower! Everything was falling in place, until...someone told us we should "check out Sun City Center, just up the road". We did.

We liked everything we saw at Sun City Center, however Peg Alway's little Fitness Center was the selling point for us! It consisted of four treadmills, two 'lo-boy' and two 'hi-boy' rowers, a stationary bicycle, a single piece of Nautilus Equipment and other 'muscle builders'. It sold us on Sun City Center! We sold our property in Sarasota, my rowing machine, and the stationary bike, and moved in to Sun City Center in June, 1987.

The Fitness Center moved to a new location in the Town Hall complex shortly after and Peg Alway became ill. Martha Lower, then on the CA Board, asked if I would take over Peg's fitness project where she devoted so much time. I agreed, and wound up in charge for two years, including the move to the Fitness Center's current location. I was proud to carry on what Peg Alway had envisioned, and I am proud of what others have done since my departure. In October, 2001, I had completed fourteen years as a Monitor in the Fitness Center.

Pat and I love Sun City Center. We have been involved with various volunteer activities including, Good Samaritan Services, Security Patrol, South Bay Hospital, Meals on Wheels, to name a few. Our hearts however, will always be at the Fitness Center which we attend five times each week. That's what brought us here in the first place, and that's what will influence a continued healthy relationship, which should keep us here for a spell.

Why We Chose Sun City Center as our Retirement Location

Ken Barringer, Ph.D.

Back in the early 1990's, my wife and I started looking for our retirement location. We wanted to make the right choice because we knew it would have a great impact on the quality of our life in our senior years. Our first efforts were devoted to gathering lots of information, but the major thrust was to schedule actual visits to key locations throughout the country.

We traveled to San Diego, Los Angeles and San Francisco. The west coast did not appeal to us because of the distance from our Sheboygan, Wisconsin location, near where many of our family are located. In Phoenix, Flagstaff and Tucson, the hot desert climate would be a problem for the summer months especially. Fort Worth and Dallas were nice, and even the eastern Texas seaboard, was attractive, but the lifestyle there just did not appeal to us.

Our best impressions were with the retirement communities of Tennessee and Arkansas, but we had no close friends or family there. Our daughter and son-in-law wanted us to settle somewhere in the research triangle area of North Carolina. Fortunately, the very week we stayed in the Raleigh-Durham area, a freak sleet and ice storm hit which totally shut it down. We asked ourselves: "Do we want to be here, especially when they have not developed retirement communities like they have in Florida that meet our standards?"

Finally, we decided to give Florida our full attention. We did go to the Villages at Lady Lake and we looked around the Venice area, where we had friends located. Then we made our second visit to Sun City Center...and we were hooked. The reason we were so sure after all this looking was that our new community fulfilled all the criteria that we had slowly been developing over all the years in our search. It was the ideal match between what we really wanted for ourselves and the kind of persons the community wanted in new homeowners.

Our Criteria for Selecting a Retirement Location might be helpful to others looking for their place under the sun. If you are already located here, however, it may make you even happier that you picked this place for your long-term future. The list below describes what we wanted in the area where we were to make our home for the rest of our lives. Sun City Center seemed to have the best combination of factors that we have found anywhere else in America. The area location has many appealing features:

1. All levels of care, from total independence to full dependence, depending on our personal circumstances.
2. It is located near a major metropolitan area and airport, and full-service medical facilities.
3. It has more options for choice of activities than we can choose, but the options are always available to us.
4. There are numerous educational opportunities in the area for personal growth geared to seniors.

5. The community has available for us many churches, and the churches work together in an Interfaith Council of congregations.
6. The area has stable and dependable community leadership and a governing body that works well with the building developer.
7. There is good, consistent weather throughout the year and sufficient rainfall to feed the environment.
8. There is a variety of housing options available for every interest and a commercial development that offers most of the necessary services needed.
9. The whole community has close, supportive and friendly neighborhoods.
10. There is an abundance of residents who express a high level of satisfaction with their choice of location. They like it here.

When we have gone back to visit our adult children and grandchildren in the Midwest, we are occasionally chided by our neighbors with the words, "Why do you want to leave paradise?" They are really saying that life here is so good that they question why we want to leave it <u>for the whole summer</u>. It's nice to know so many people we meet feel this way, even after 40 years of development. Maybe it has taken us all these years to get our act together so we have learned to just get it right. Now we can truly enjoy the fruits of our efforts and planning. That happens every day!

Twenty-Five Years in Sun City Center
by Harriet Radebaugh

We first heard of Sun City Center while having lunch with friends in a small village in southern New Jersey. When asked what we planned to do on retirement we said we were moving to Clearwater, Florida. "Oh no", said our friend. You must go to Sun City Center. They had bought a house there while waiting for his retirement.

A long time later, while getting ready for our vacation, we began getting phone calls from a salesman wanting us to spend five days and four nights as his guest in Sun City Center. We decided to take him up on his offer, and stay one day and one night.

Driving down Route 41, we wondered at all those huge phosphate dunes on the west side of the road. We decided this wasn't going to be any place for us driving along the two-lane route 674 with all the junk cars, shacks and a decrepit restaurant called "Big Daddy's" which, incidentally, we later found to be THE place to eat! We then came to a little oasis.

After registering at the Inn and calling the salesman, we were ready to see what this place was all about. We toured the homes, played a round of golf on both courses and bought a lot. We drove around the plot of ground that was filled with trees and we were told there was to be a beautiful lake in the middle. We kept turning that little piece of paper until we ended up with a corner lot, facing northeast, avoiding the afternoon sun. Selling our Michigan home was next on the agenda.

We received a phone call telling us the "lake" was in, and we didn't have any better sense than to fly down to see it. We didn't know if we should laugh or cry when seeing that hole in the ground with about 2 feet of water and a row boat. It wasn't long before we found it was a "holding pond," not a lake, but it provides a nice view from our family room.

When the house was completed, I moved in as Carl still had a month left to work and the house in Michigan still had to be sold. It was a month of frustration as many things weren't right, but finally Carl arrived and things looked much brighter. We had furnished the place on one of our trips down, so our next big item was buying a golf cart. That meant selling my pretty yellow sports car, but we needed the room in the car port.

More or less settled in, the next business was getting tee times. The procedure at the North Course, as it was known then, involved being over there by 6:30 AM (or earlier) and getting in line to draw a bingo ball. Tee times were given in order of the number on that little ball. A high number and you might as well go home. I felt so sorry one day for the man who drew Number 1, and then accidentally dropped it, and never got it back in the mad scramble! To get a tee time on the South Course (now called the Sandpiper) you called on the phone in the morning – and practically wore out the dial trying to get a line, but persistence would pay off eventually.

We both became involved in the golf leagues and soon found the Kings and Queens. As all old-time golfers know, that took up every Monday of the year, rain or shine. A scramble in the morning, cocktail parties around four, and dinner at the Inn. I was on the Board for the 18-hole Ladies League, and Carl was on the board for the 18-hole Men's League. I also joined the Emergency Squad as an Expediter; that was in the days before we served Kings Point. One fund drive, people were asked to put white pillow cases on their lamp post if they were willing to donate. Squad members then canvassed the neighborhoods in golf carts collecting money (and pillow cases).

Sitting in Ceramics class one day, we were asked if any of us wanted to go poolside and have our pictures taken with Caesar Romero. He was there making a video for promotional purposes for WG, the company developing both Sun City Center and Kings Point at the time. He even honored us by coming to our Kings and Queens dinner that night.

Another lady in ceramics and I started a China Painting Club with five members. We met in each other's homes. Eventually, we got a club room although at first we could only use it at night – but that was scary with no outside lights in that area. I've participated in many clubs here, and enjoyed them all.

It has been interesting to watch the area grow although some of us miss the earlier small-town atmosphere. It seemed at one time that we knew everyone here but, with passage of time, so many of our long-time friends are gone. I was recently asked by a visitor if I like it here. I told her I'd been here 25 years. She replied, "Well, I guess you do."

A First Impression -- "Not for Us" But on Second Thought -- "Let's Join Them"

Phil Lange

It was in 1970 that we received the kind of pictured greeting card that lured many SCC residents to this Mecca. The last sentence said, "And next time you're in Florida be sure to visit us." Well, we were scheduled for a national conference in Miami. But where was Sun City Center? Map reading located it near Tampa, a long way from Miami. That would mean travel by car from New Jersey instead of by plane.

Routed by AAA on US highway 41 to Ruskin, we found the turn onto State Highway 674, a narrow two-lane road that took us to The Kings Inn and the Sun City Center sign. While parking at the Inn, the first eight humans we saw included two pedaling tricycles, two using wheelchairs, and four in golf carts. No one on foot. No place for us!

But noting our out-of-state license, all made a point of saying hello or greetings. And inside the Inn there was a riot of fellowship and endless where-are-you-from conversation.

Early the next morning we located our friends' home on Costa Street; but it lacked the mountain in the background that had been pictured on their postcard. (How much else was fake?) The Newells had timed our visit to coincide with the Costa Street home owners' party, with layers and layers of praise for the good and easy life of Sun City Center...and the owners' testimony about their co-op management creating reality for a northern snow-bird's dream.

Three weeks later, back in New Jersey, we got a phone call from a Costa Street resident, saying, "I've got one of those Spanish 2-story villas for sale. What do you say?"

"Let's join them" had easily displaced "not for us."

How Did I Get Here and Why Did I Stay?

Paul Robbins

Many SCC residents have an interesting story to tell as to how they happened to come to our town. There are dozens of reasons as to why they stayed.

My wife and I were staying for a few days at Bahia Beach Resort in 1971 when one of the other guests remarked, "Sun City Center retirement community in as interesting place to visit." We drove over and visited SCC for a couple of hours. We were most impressed with its well-kept yards, the many lakes and the old codgers zipping around in their golf carts.

The next year on our Florida vacation we tried the east coast and fell in love with a resort in Vero Beach. We returned to Vero Beach for usually two weeks each year for the next 10 years.

In the spring of 1982 I took my wife to Mayo Clinic in Rochester for a checkup. While visiting a men's room there, I got in a conversation with a man. When he said he was from SCC, Florida, I remembered my short stop there. Since I was retiring the following January, we were now looking for a five to six months' home in Florida.

I asked the SCC man if he thought we could rent a place there for the winter. He thought there was a good chance to do so, and gave me the name of a Realtor. The Realtor was able to find us an almost new duplex on Bluewater Drive. We loved it and rented another place for the following winter before going north in the spring. Meanwhile we kept looking for a home we wanted to buy, and bought it the second winter here.

It was not difficult to find reasons to make this our home. We loved the warm winters and the opportunity to be out of doors almost every day. I enjoyed working in the yard and soon had a grove of six citrus trees in the back yard. I enjoyed golf, did some lawn bowling, shuffleboard and even pitched some horseshoes. The swimming pools and walking pool are marvelous. Bridge in SCC is outstanding. We were really impressed with the free services of the Emergency Squad. The very low crime rate due, at least in part, by the work of the Security Patrol, encouraged us to be a part of this organization.

However I am an educator, having spent about 36 years as a college professor. Education moved me as an underpriviledged youth from the other side of the tracks to the land of opportunity. Many communities in Florida offer great opportunities for golf, swimming, bridge, crafts, etc. However I was interested in intellectual stimulation as well as golf and bridge. I also found that in Community Church College and in various programs such as Issues and Ideas and Coffee and Conversation.

The College, run primarily by volunteers, offers 40 to 50 non-credit courses each year in the fall and again in the spring semester. This continuing education outreach program serves the entire community and surrounding areas. The purpose of the College is to inform and to inspire. A broad curriculum of subjects is offered. All courses are taught by highly qualified instructors drawn primarily from the local community.

I have been very involved with the College and other educational activities since arriving in SCC in January of 1983. I feel most fortunate that I have been here. I am so glad I talked with the SCC gentleman at Mayo Clinic men's room in Rochester. I wish I could remember his name so I could thank him.

Sun City Center - An Adventure Into Retirement

Ewing E. Smith

It was 1976 when we began to think of retirement. Our thoughts ran to islands in the Caribbean. Trips to Hilton Head, Marco Island, Orlando and Deltona put these attractive spots under consideration also.

Having braved the severe winters of Pennsylvania and New York for many years, our thinking was to choose an area that would be pleasant year round, away from cosmopolitan areas, but near enough to a city to allow us to enjoy its amenities.

A retired superintendent of schools and a former associate came to visit us and gave such a glowing report of Del Webb's concept of retirement living that we had to satisfy our curiosity about it. In 1971 we first visited Sun City Center.

On our first three visits we stayed at King's Inn. Our evening walks took us up streets impressively lighted by house post lights. Balmy breezes, swaying palms silhouetted above us by a bright moon made our walks enchanting. Of course, catching glimpses of private parties at the inn, with couples in their finery, gave one a feeling of wanting to be part of this wonderful life. We found that golf, swimming, bridge and theater were available for the taking, and plenty of cultural activities and fine restaurants in nearby Tampa. Who could ask for anything more?

It was in 1981 that we made the move to Sun City Center and have enjoyed an abundant and most enjoyable life since then.

Our Son Brought Us To Sun City Center

Mary Lou Munro

We had moved four years earlier from Ohio to Surfside Beach, SC and believed we were settled for life - many great golf courses, one mile from the beach, and a beautiful town house on Deer Track Golf Course.

Alex had attended a golf school on the premises and thought he had found Paradise. In the meantime, our younger son, Scott, had relocated from Ohio to Florida and was urging his father to come down and check out the super golf courses on the Gulf Coast. After several trips and visits to courses up and down the West Coast of Florida, we agreed that maybe it was time to make a move - again. The thought of leaving our South Carolina paradise was painful, but we finally decided to look for a place near Tampa. We were led to Sun City Center by the golf facilities and the beauty of the residential area - well-kept homes, green grass, and friendly neighbors. In October we made the big move and have never regretted it.

We both concentrated mainly on golf for a few years, and I soon found other interests as well. The community newspaper was of special interest to me and I was a member of the staff for over 8 years, serving as Managing Director for the last seven. I was also involved in several local and county government committees. Life was good and we were enjoying every minute of it.

GOD HAD BROUGHT US TO SUN CITY CENTER FOR A REASON

Then tragedy struck in 1991, and we realized that God had brought us to Sun City Center for a reason. Our son was diagnosed with melanoma on his brain, and we became part of his support system. Though he fought gallantly for almost two years, we ultimately lost him and were grateful for the many good times we had shared together. We thank God that, in his wisdom, he led us here, not only for Scott's sake but also because of the love and support within the community.

This became even more apparent to me two years ago when I lost Alex to leukemia. I have never felt alone, still maintain my own house, and carry on the activities I so enjoy. My son Alex III, who lives in California, tells me that if I didn't live in Sun City Center, he couldn't leave me here alone. I'm convinced there is no better retirement community than Sun City Center!

A Quick Decision and The Right One

Marian Armstrong

In 1976, while I was vacationing in St. Armond's Key, my future husband drove down from New Jersey to see me. Someone mentioned Sun City Center and our curiosity was piqued. We drove to this most beautiful oasis, married, and moved here in October of '76.

The first thing we did was to sign up to help with Meals on Wheels in order to get to know the town. Later we joined the Security Patrol. Meanwhile, Bob enjoyed his game of golf while I made changes and decorated our home.

We both have been active in clubs and in the Community Association. Bob was elected to the board and served as its President during much of the formulating time of the 1984 Agreement with the developer of Sun City Center. I can't imagine living anywhere else. We've had a life here of fulfillment in so many ways.

Everything is here! Get involved! We did, and the friends, personal satisfaction and memories we have are precious.

It Was Meant To Be

Nan Dorsey

Our youngest child had just graduated from college, Jack had just retired, and we were visiting many Florida retirement communities. Jack had sent for videos and we were working our way down the coast. We purchased a lot in Ocala, signed a contract for a home to be built, and headed to Sarasota to visit friends. We had lived in Sarasota for several years in the early 80's and loved the area. One of our friends was president of a large manufacturing plant in Sarasota. At dinner one evening, he asked Jack if he would be willing to work for just a year to help vitalize the sales and marketing department. We all felt we were young enough to postpone retirement and agreed. We looked forward to returning to Sarasota.

Next, dear friends of ours, who had built just south of the Sun City Center exit, extended a dinner invitation. We were looking forward to visiting and catching up on the lives of our respective children, grandchildren and with each other. Just before the exit, Jack reminded me that our young friends were still working. Our invitation was for 6:00, and it was just 4:00, so we decided to pop into Sun City Center's Welcome Center, have an orange drink and cookie, and look around. At 6:00 we telephoned our friends from the sales office explaining that we had just signed a purchase agreement for a new home! The rest is history. We have enjoyed seven years here.

We have looked back many times. We find Sun City Center a real hometown of caring, talented and intelligent neighbors. The extraordinary folks who volunteer to keep our town growing are from all walks of life. If anyone could have guessed how busy one might be in retirement, it wouldn't have been me. We find all kinds of different resources available here to maintain, enjoy and promote a healthy lifestyle. As one of the Realtors told us, we don't just sell property in Sun City Center, we offer a great way of life. And, for us, it was meant to be.

All In The Family

Eleanore Chase

Never in my wildest dreams had I ever planned to live in Florida. In fact, I had planned *not* to. When my husband, Hal, was released from duty at the Naval Air Station in Miami at war's end, we high-tailed it back to the beautiful rolling hills of Pennsylvania as fast as we could go.

If it hadn't been for Hal's dad and his wife, Phoebe, we wouldn't be here now. They had traded their little farm in upstate New York, with its blustery snowy winters, for the comfort of Florida retirement. As traveling became increasingly difficult for them, we took to spending one of our vacation weeks in central Florida with them every year.

Somehow our perception of flat Florida changed as its solid groves of oranges and grapefruit began to include the inviting look of residential development. A few years later, as we neared retirement age, we decided to visit my Aunt Wenna who lived in a little town west of us called Sun City Center. With map in hand, we set off north on route 301 and turned left on route 674. It was such a nice surprise to see the rows of adorable little homes with beautifully manicured lawns along Rickenbacker Drive. We passed the Sun City Center Inn and the shopping center and "Oh look! They seem to have everything you need here -- one gas station, one drug store, a barber shop, a Chinese Restaurant, a furniture store and a small Winn Dixie." We passed a bank and there, on our left, was the sign we were looking for, "Kings Point," our final destination.

When I look back, it was that very day that changed our lives completely. Aunt Wenna begged us to stay long enough for her to show off her town that she had chosen after much research. The more we saw the more convinced we became that we had found the perfect retirement community. By this time we wanted nothing more than to escape our Pennsylvania winters.

Remember, I'm reminiscing. All this was back in 1981, over twenty years ago. Sun City Center has grown so fast it boggles my mind with the changes. Our two-lane route 674 is now four lanes with islands of palm trees and flowers, and edged with streetlights. There are more and more beautiful homes to choose from and many people opt to "house hop" as their lifestyle changes from being in a second home to full-time living. We, however, decided on a little house on Middle Lake to which we have added a dining room, a third bedroom, a study for Hal, a couple of bay windows and a pool. With all this we are very happy to stay put.

One does not have to be a bridge or golf aficionado. With so many activities offered here, one can't help but keep busy. In fact, we keep so busy it is hard to find time for an afternoon nap!

Times do change. I remember that first Sunday while looking around during church I thought, "Oh, goodness, all those gray heads! What are we doing here?" But the time flies. We are now entering our eighties and I got to thinking at church last Sunday, that we are sure blending with the gray heads, and that we have loved every minute of these last twenty years.

It was a happy day for us when we decided so long ago to visit Aunt Wenna. And the story repeats itself. Hal's brother and his wife and sister and her husband surprised us last year. After visits, and liking what they saw, both families have bought retirement homes here.

Never in my wildest dreams did I think I would be living in Florida and now never in my wildest dreams could I imagine living anywhere else.

Hal and Eleanore

Why Sun City Center?

Byron Deming

My story begins in 1990 when my wife died in Rocklyn, California. I lived on the top of a hill overlooking about nine small cities. After being a widower for a year or so, listening to soft music and watching the sun go down, my recently widowed sister signed me up for an Elderhostel in San Diego. By then I had put everything in storage, sold my home and moved my batchelorhood into my RV to continue exploration of the remainder of the United States.

At the Elderhostel, I met Carolyn, a widow, and explained that I was one of those poor homeless ones you read about. After completing our short Elderhostel education in computers, astronomy and public artwork, Carolyn and I parted -- she to her magnificent home in Albany, New York, and me to my homeless life of a vagabond.

A short time later, on one of our phone calls, she mentioned there was another Elderhostel coming up in Florida soon and inquired if I was going. I replied that the timing was poor for I was returning to Costa Rica, and would she join me? We agreed on some ground rules and she accepted that invitation like a cat on catnip, due to her insatiable appetite for travel, particularly foreign travel. After returning from Costa Rica we toured the U.S. in my RV. When we got to Florida, Carolyn mentioned she had an old friend living in Sun City Center.

After a couple of drinks, her old friend Thomas Muir and his wife Char gave us the hard sell on Sun City Center that ended with a tour in his golf cart of a new section called Villas on the Green that was just opening a few blocks from him. The streets were in, but there was nothing else but dirt. He showed us his choice for a lot and recommended a new model home with a loft in it. I knew he had good judgment, since I agreed with all his opinions.

The next day I got serious with the builder and the deal was done. Initially I wanted to buy a lot and build my own home, but we finally settled on the model I had admired. Several lively conversations with the builder followed (expletives deleted). At least we were on the golf course, the pond and an agreement that I could build a pool. For 101 days we watched our home being built while living in the RV in Siesta Grove RV Park in Palmetto. In 1994, Carolyn recorded the date in the wet cement driveway.

When the house was done, it was time to move in. I had the advantage since all my worldly goods were packed away in storage in California and ready to be moved on a moment's notice. Otherwise, we would have had a severe problem since Carolyn had a large home in Albany (about 4,000 square feet) and my last home had about 4,000 square feet too. In the Navy that's what was referred to as a "blivette", which is 10 pounds of crap in a five-pound bag. Carolyn off-loaded much on her children, but still pays storage bills in New York and Palmetto.

We moved in with the firm understanding that I don't garden and I don't paint. I am a man of my word which is easy since Carolyn loves to garden and paint. In no time she had planted an additional eleven palm trees and a small oasis by the golf course.

And they lived happily ever after.

From New York to Djakarta to Florida

Len Perry

The cold weather in February '80 did it for me. I had suffered a major heart attack while working in Djakarta, Indonesia. My rehab, among other things, was walking. But the cold, frigid weather in New York was very troubling trying to maintain a schedule. Result: my cardiologist said "warmer climate."

Okay, we thought about going west, maybe New Mexico or California. When our children heard what we were thinking they advised us that the distance would be hard on the families. We should consider the south, such as Florida. No way. We had been going to Fort Lauderdale for fifteen years to visit both Elaine's and my parents. Besides, to my thinking, the east coast was "New York with palm trees." The congestion, all the people - no way was Florida on our agenda. But to please our children, we acquiesced.

We traveled for three weeks all over the state, to Jacksonville, Tequesta, Orlando, New Port Richey, Tarpon Springs - you name it, we were there. We were on our way back to Tarpon Springs after visiting my parents on the east coast when we stopped in Bradenton for a cup of coffee. Elaine had a book from our local library titled "Retirement in the Sun Belt" and noted "a community named Sun City Center was just north of Bradenton off US 41."

We proceeded north, saw a sign for "Sun City" and went in, but it was not what was described in the book. Needless to say, we eventually saw another sign and we proceeded on SR 674, a two-lane road, to this little town of 5,000. What a beautiful sight - an oasis in the middle of nowhere. We both immediately knew that this would be our new community.

The developer at the time was W/G and they put us in the Inn for three days to "look over the town." Elaine and I, along with Realtor Trudy Coleman, found the dwelling we have called "home" these many wonderful years. We rented while our area was being cleared for development and I proceeded with my walking schedule. Amazingly I found that I had no problem walking 3-4 miles every day and I never once had to use the "nitro" that I carried. I felt great. Indeed, this was the place for Elaine and me.

Elaine was very careful that I did not over extend my limits and she would tell me to "take it easy, you are retired." Little did I know what she had been told about my heart. The "attack" had done major damage and the cardiologist told her I had a two-year life expectancy. They hadn't told me that, and I was running around like a happy camper. Sixteen years later I underwent a quadruple bypass.

Meanwhile my neighbor, Bud Miller, President of the Homeowners' Association, was charged by the Civic Association to develop a plan to stop the burglaries in town. He invited me to join this small group -- we met at Gigi Giordano's house and that was the start of our great Security Patrol. I was Captain of Team 26, Assistant Chief, Deputy Chief of Operations, Group Leader, Board Member and President.

When South Bay Hospital opened, Elaine and I signed on as volunteers and, eventually served on the Volunteer Advisory Council. We were volunteers for about ten years there.

I have found so many warm, caring and energetic people in our community that makes us so unique. I had a vision of American Flags flying along SR 674 and mentioned it to Bob Saxon of the Lions Club, Ed Socha of TROA, the Executive Director of the Chamber of Commerce at that time and Lyle Thomas of WCI Communities. Putting their combined talents together resulted in Sun City Center being the first community in the state to fly American Flags on a state road. Generous donations to our Flag Fund, "Proudly We Hail" by our residents have enabled the flag program to continue now for several years.

I have kept busy with many civic groups; I chair "Hi, Neighbor!", serve as a director of the Community Association and during the 22 years we have lived here, have been on many boards and councils such as Prince of Peace, Interfaith, American Legion and Veterans of Foreign Wars -- and I could not have been with a finer group anywhere!

I found what Ponce de Leon was looking for -- but then again, Del Webb was not around.

Why We Moved to Sun City Center

by Marge and Cornell Clarke

During the 1980's, Cornell and I spent part of February and March at Anna Marie Island in Holmes Beach. In 1986 we drove to Sun City Center to visit friends that we knew from Fairfield, Iowa where we had lived for ten years. The guys took Cornell golfing and the gals and I caught up on each other, and we had lunch and dinner together! The next year we repeated our fun day together in Sun City Center.

In 1988, Sun City Center had a special! For $88.00 you could spend a weekend in the Golf Villas, use all the facilities, including the Racquet Club and a round of golf. We took them up on this wonderful offer and had a fabulous weekend.

In 1989, we were able to rent a home for four months for what it cost us for six weeks in Holmes Beach. Who could resist?

Needless to say, I was fascinated with the thought that I could drive all over town in a golf cart and I wanted to learn shell crafting, plus there were so many other crafts available. We were excited about lawn bowling, and it just seemed like a wonderful place to retire.

We bought a small house before going back to Kentucky, thinking we would go back and forth each year. That lasted two years before we decided life was so great here, why go back to the gray days in Kentucky when we could enjoy the sunshine here and new friends. Besides, Cornell bought me my Sun-City-Center-Cadillac that he had promised me for years, my golf cart! Now I enjoy driving it and talking on my cell phone on the way to the Racquet Club for water aerobics and whatever!

IT STARTED WITH A WEEK OF SUNDAYS
by **Ina Coplan**
(As told to Tricia Smith)

In 1981, as a blessed break from teaching school, Ina and Burt decided to accept an invitation from Realtor, Trudy Coleman, to stay here a week to get acquainted with Sun City Center. They stayed in a little place near the firehouse and loved everything they saw. They were not at that time ready to retire but several years later they had eliminated other possible towns that they visited and were back again to choose their future home here.

There was nothing but cow pasture south of Flamingo and development stopped at Allegheny on the north side. The Plaza contained the small Winn Dixie, a travel agency, a tiny post office and a theater which showed Spanish films in the main. The developer was building in the Bluewater area and the Coplans chose Cactus Flower Drive as their location. They came, complete with a 24 foot sailboat, in 1983 and moaned a few moans because the light from the telephone relay tower on East Del Webb shone right into their bedroom at night. The boat found a home at a marina in nearby Bahia Beach and Ina and Bert immediately found themselves at home in Sun City Center, getting involved with the Civic Association, the Homeowners' Association and the Interfaith Council. Burt became the second President of the Council. Recycling was a big fund-raising vehicle at that time. Everyone participated, taking their bottles, newspapers and other collectibles to the waiting trailer every Saturday. The Nearly New Shop started at that time and, as we know, it is still a formidable money- maker for the Council.

The Jewish Community bought a parcel of land designated for building a temple. For 9 years they had worshipped at the United Community Church, at the kind invitation of Pastor Robert Gingery, until the present temple was completed. To thank the church members the Jewish congregation commissioned Grace Barrett, a local sculptress, to do a head of Moses for their church.

When "Herbie" Sage was Chancellor of the Community Church College, Ina became Dean, with her special duty to find teachers and programs.

At that time there were only three tennis courts but a tennis club was formed and she became active not only at the game but also socially. Ina was reminiscing about the pleasant social life of the early '80s. "Saturdays were very special. The "Kings and Queens," a group of two hundred golfers, played golf Monday mornings. Then there were cocktail parties from five to seven, very formally by invitation, and everyone went to the Inn for dinner. Tea dances took place every Sunday. Everyone knew each other. They looked after each other. It was so intimate that the residents were totally opposed to widening 674. "Don't make it easy for outside people to get here," they laughingly said.

Ina is experiencing that feeling of intimacy again, having moved into the Independent Living section of the Courtyards. She is surrounded by caring friends and personnel and still loving living in Sun City Center.

My Dream Came True

Janet Fischesser

The sunny skies and warm breezes beckoned when my sister suggested we drive down to visit several friends wintering in sunny Florida in the winter of 1980. We scouted out several spots, thinking of retiring in the near future. Not being fully satisfied in St. Petersburg or Clearwater, we decided to have lunch with friends in a place named Sun City Center.

As soon as I passed the fountains at the entrance, I knew this was the place for me. We had lunch on Costa Street (my first residence was a rental on that street) and sought out several more long-time family friends who had moved here recently. They insisted that we spend a few days at the Inn and do a little research. It didn't take me long to become convinced that I had found the haven I was looking for – no doubt about it, this was the spot. However, I had nine more working years before I could make the transition.

Luck was certainly with me. A good friend phoned the following summer to let me know she had given up her residency in Sarasota and bought a place in Kings Point. I was delighted. The following year, to put the icing on the cake, my brother called to let me know he had played golf in a 'small community' in Florida, liked it, and bought a house. You guessed it – Sun City Center.

My dream came true. I retired in 1989, sold my house in Cincinnati, and moved here in May of 1990. I believe it was the best decision I ever made. I've been more than happy with the many amenities offered in this area, and especially satisfied that I never have to shovel snow.

"It's an ill wind"

by Don Pagano

This is an expression much used in its widest sense by people generally. It is an abbreviation for the saying 'It's an ill wind that blows no one some good.' and simply means however unfavorable conditions may be, there is always someone or something that will benefit from them.

That someone was me and the benefit was landing here in Sun City Center. But let me start at the beginning.

I had just recently returned to Miami where three of my children were located. I had rented an apartment centrally located near them. The amenities were just what I wanted, use of a swimming pool, tennis court and etc.

But then along came the "Ill Wind" the infamous hurricane "Andrew". It devastated my apartment building and it was uninhabitable. My children had considerable damage to their homes as well. With no decent place to stay I got in my car which had been spared and traveled north. I was able to find a cousin of mine who lived in Winter Haven. I stayed with her and her husband for a time.

I then looked up a former associate of mine Curtis Keeler who I worked with at Eastern Airlines as Flight Ground School instructors teaching pilots to operate jet aircraft. I had not seen him in ten years. He now lived in Sun City Center.

He graciously invited me to his home for a weekend and gave me a tour of the facilities. I was able to play some tennis with some residents who were complete strangers but who welcomed me and enabled me to experience the friendliness and warmth that is the trademark of Sun City Center residents.

It was then I decided to live in Sun City Center. I joined the Tennis Association and the wonderful friends I have made here since has been so gratifying. I also joined the computer club. Since I had experience with computers I volunteered to instruct beginner's classes and found that to be a rewarding experience.

All in all I would have to say the "Ill wind" that blew me north to Sun City Center is the silver lining in the clouds of the storm.

You'll be Surprised What Drew Me Here
by John Manning

Believe it or not, I came to Sun City Center because of the sidewalks!

My wife, Carolyn, and I had this house built from the ground up for a special reason: ramps, light switches accessible from a wheelchair—sidewalks to keep me off the road.

I don't play golf, tennis, bowl, or any other "extreme" sport. But I was able to participate in plenty of the community's activities. There were a number of people "in high places" who didn't want "handicaps" living in Sun City Center—and flagrantly said so—but most folks made me feel welcome.

In fact, members of the Men's Club began actively working with me and other people in wheelchairs to fund construction of electric doors in many parts of the community. That touched my heart, and I never go through one of those doors that I don't think of the kindness that has been shown.

Our Retirement Life In Kings Point

Lil Upperman

We moved to Kings Point in 1983 after selling our Dairy Queen business in Ohio. In the previous years we had been coming down to Florida during the winter months, staying in Sarasota on the Gulf Coast side, so we knew this area quite well. We decided to choose Kings Point in Sun City Center as our permanent home because it offered the most for what we needed and for what we wanted.

We have a moderate size home in a duplex and my husband's sister lives next door as our roof neighbor. We love people so, before we know it, we have acquired many good friends besides our neighbors.

I like to cook. Sometimes I invite our friends to our house for dinners. I would spend hours making authentic Italian dishes and desserts. Everyone praised me for being such an excellent cook, except my husband. He is basically a meat and potato man, and we have been married for fifty-nine years.

We love to play card games, and we invite our friends to play with us. The games like most are Double Domino, Mexican Train, Rummikub, Royal Rummy or other games according to Hoyle. We played these games in different homes almost every week.

The good part of living in Kings Point has been that we could do our regular exercise in walking, even walking after dark. We feel safe because we live in a gated community. There are guards on duty twenty-four hours a day. I swim in the indoor and outdoor pools, and we use the exercise and fitness room that is full of all sorts of machines and equipment. I also ride a tricycle bike.

My husband, Lefty, and I love to dance Ballroom. We took dance lessons and joined the Kings Point Dance Club. In our magnificent auditorium, the parquet floor is great for dancing. We dance with live music and with a big band. We also participate in the dances held in Sun City Center. There are many opportunities to dance, until your feet hurt!! In recent years, Lefty has been running dance practice sessions with taped music in the Health Room. We practice Fox-Trot, Waltz, Rumba Bolero, Cha-Cha, Swing, Quickstep, and more!

The Kings Point auditorium has a showcase stage equipped with sophisticated light and sound system allowing for big events and productions to be presented. Like the Sun City Center Follies, The Ms. Senior Sun City Center Pageant, Pelican Players productions, Swing Band concerts, K.P. Mixed Voices Chorus, Good Samaritan Ball, Halloween Dance and New Years Party. The stage and facilities attract many top-billing entertainers and performers to appear each year, and there are big-screen movies shown weekly.

Lefty is an avid fisherman and owned an 18-foot powerboat with trailer. Kings Point provided the space for storage when it was not in use. Lefty and his fishing buddies regularly pulled the boat to Bahia Beach and Simmons Park just a few miles away and would fish all along the coastline of Tampa Bay. Some days they would catch, clean and fillet flounder, sea bass, sheepshead and other species for me to cook or put in the freezer. Lefty likes to tell the story of how the biggest one got away.

Another pleasurable activity I did with my friends was to pick strawberries, blueberries, peppers and tomatoes. Sun City Center is surrounded by fields and farms, and the three major crops are tomatoes, citrus products and strawberries. Harvest time attracts many migrant farm workers to this area and, after the commercial picking is finished, the fields are opened to the public. We girls looked forward to picking - it gave us time to talk and get away from housework and chores.

In Kings Point, we are happy with our retirement life, and we are content and satisfied with the lot that has been given us. Our only prayer is that our good health will hold out.

Lil and Lefty

We've Moved !

John Bowker

Our dear Wendy, John and Dan,

By now our news shouldn't surprise you but, indeed, mom and I have bought and moved into our new home in Sun City Center, Florida! We can't wait for each of you to come down to see our new digs.

We had told the Realtor we wanted a three-bedroom house on a lake, facing the south or west with no windows in the front, a two-car garage, and one story construction. We figured we could sit out back by the water without the sun beating down on us and the house could be easily cooled. What *really* surprised us was, when we arrived for our visit, she was able to show us five houses all exactly as we had described. And wouldn't you know it, we selected and bought a sixth one that had just come on the market! It is 12 years old, we're the third owner, so we know all the kinks will have been worked out by our predecessors.

It's truly a treasure with an enormous master bedroom, with two other "bedrooms"; one to answer mom's need for a bright sewing center (it looks out over the lake), and another will be perfect for my computer and radio hobbies. Mom is already painting all the inside walls -- 26 gallons of paint! (You talk about carpel tunnel syndrome!) I have been busy with important things like making sure the cable tv works in all the rooms, and cleaning a spare refrigerator that had been unplugged for months but was still full of "frozen" food. (yecch!)

We weren't in the house a full day before one of the neighbors tapped on the door to say hello and to tell us that a neighbor had noticed our name on the lamp post (like everybody else here). She had once known a "John Bowker" and he was dating a girl named "Linda" but that was nearly a half century ago and happened in a small town in Vermont. We both nearly fainted! Turns out she was our high-school physics teacher in 1947. And just three blocks away, we learned of another Middlebury man -- he and I were playmates some 50+ years ago.

Yesterday two things happened; a man from the volunteer Security Patrol visited us and we agreed to join in the patrol that keeps an eye on things, "anything that looks like it doesn't quite belong here" were his words. And in the afternoon I attended the monthly

Amateur Radio Club meeting -- they asked if I would become Secretary next year ... and I will probably say “yes.”

We’re just 20 minutes from the beach and there’s a neat restaurant right there; we’re told the water temperature is in the low 80s in the summer, so you can guess where we’ll be much of the time.

But we can’t wait for you and all our grandchildren to come see this fine place. It’s just like summer here all year round ... we’re about two hours from Mr. Disney’s empire and with the 100+ activity clubs, we’ll probably just run out of time! Tell your kids that grandma and grandpa have found a place to live where they don’t have to work and they can go out and play everyday just like they do during the summer when school is closed. It’s true!

All our love,

M and D

Louise Hutt
(97 years young)

When my husband and I arrived on December 12, 1966 the road from Ruskin was lined with shacks, cattle and dumps. We had to travel this road as there was no bank, no store.

Our one doctor, Dr. Wentzell, was wonderful. He made house calls. There was no hospital, no fire department or equipment.

Mr. Del Webb flew in, landing on a small area south of road 674. He was a golfer and often visited to tee off. There were no homes south of 674 and none north of Allegheny.

DR. ROBERT GINGERY, INNOVATOR
As told to Tricia Smith

Dr. Gingery with his wife, Betty, came to Sun City Center to visit his parents, liked it and lo and behold he came back as Senior Minister to the United Community Church in 1972. His parents are no longer living but he has three older sisters, two of whom own homes on Swan Lake and two younger brothers who also live in Sun City Center.

When Dr. and Mrs. Gingery moved here he looked on this new ministry as a great opportunity to experiment. Everybody came from somewhere else. He thought of everyone, including himself, in the light of the Pilgrims, who arrived in a brand new home looking for freedom of religion and a new life of volunteerism.

Dr. Gingery told with amusement some of his early experiments, meant to illustrate a liturgical point. Borrowing from Williams College's Haystack Meeting concerning the origin of the World Mission of the Church, he ordered a load of hay to be deposited in the chancel, with the result that allergic parishioners fled sneezing from the church. Another experiment involving a pool and a large flowing fountain in the chancel prompted a suggestive run on the Church's restrooms.

Early on he met some thespians on a trip to staid old England who proposed bringing a theatrical work to the church. Sure that, being British it would be uplifting and educational he accepted their offer. Lacking a "hall" at that time, he invited them to present the theatrical piece in the chancel. It turned out to be called "No Sex, Please – We're British" quite a raunchy work which had everyone blushing, particularly the Pastor.

The church building itself had an entirely different look from today. What is now the atrium was " the outdoors," with palm trees waving. There was very little space inside for offices, library and chapel. Expansion within and modernization without were of prime importance. The Great Hall, the library and many offices and classrooms appeared in time through Dr. Gingery's vision and the collaboration of many talented parishioners.

Dr. Gingery shared his dreams with his parishioners as well as the community, many in the area of education. They shared back by participating either financially, physically or both. Edwin J. Dietz, for example, contributed a large amount to the church, dedicated to scholarships for young people in Hillsborough County. Since education was one of Dr. Gingery's main appetites he initiated the Community Church College with a modest curriculum which, through the years, has expanded its scope exponentially. The retirees of the area are both the volunteer teachers, calling on the experiences of their past specialties, and the students, who profit by new learning interests.

He investigated the problems of the poor people of Wimauma, and learning from them that their major need was assistance with housing he started the W.A.I.A.(Wimauma Area Improvement Authority). 100 homes called Newmauma Homes have been built and

maintained for low income families. This worthy program has won the support of the U.S. Government's Department of Housing and Urban Development.
With George Grange Dr. Gingery began a plan for assisting elderly or incapable residents of Sun City Center which has become a mighty force for good called the Guardianship Foundation. The members of this selfless board undertake to free their clients from financial anxiety by obtaining power of attorney and handling their financial problems devoting countless hours to their task.

. When the Jewish Community needed a place to worship temporarily, Dr. Gingery made space available in the United Community Church for as long as they needed it, even filling in as preacher on occasion. His interest in the formation of the Interfaith Social Action Council is further evidence of Dr. Gingery's concern for cooperation among all the churches in the Sun City Center, Ruskin and Wimauma areas. He also helped to organize the Sunpoint Orchestra.

Such are some of the fulfilled dreams of the thirty years of tenure of this forward thinking Pastor who made a never to be forgotten mark in the Sun City Center community. He is a religious leader whose impact always reached far beyond the membership within his church and built roots both in the local and surrounding communities. We Pilgrims appreciate his legacy.

Dr. Robert Gingery

My Story

by Jean Krause

In the fall of 1979 my husband Phil and I were considering going to Florida to look for a winter home. We lived in the beautiful Berkshires of Massachusetts, but facing another winter there was not appealing to us. We heard about Sun City Center from a friend at church whose brother was a real estate agent there.

I'll admit I really was not enthused about the idea as we were very active people, and I envisioned us sitting on a park bench, twiddling our fingers. Phil still teases me about my remark that I didn't want to go down there "with all those old people."

Well, we came, we saw, and we bought a little "doll house" on the water and the golf course in Kings Point. It was like opening a gift box—we discovered so many things to do, and with the beautiful weather as an additional gift. We thought we "had died and gone to heaven." We swam, played tennis, tutored at Wimauma Elementary School, took college courses at the United Community Church College. Phil discovered he could paint when he took some art classes, and we have some beautiful paintings to show for it. We also helped start the Kings Point Ballroom Dance Club, helped form the Academy of Ballroom Dance School, and studied dancing under the tutelage of Carl and Mary Forsberg. Later, we became student assistants.

Carl and Mary Forsberg have done so much for Sun City Center by operating this dance school since 1981. It is still as popular as ever. We treasure the friends we have made over the past twenty years that we have been associated with this school. We always enjoyed taking part in the "Follies" held at Kings Point each year. At one time I was one of the Gladys Demetrion Dancers, as well.

Back then, Rte. 674 was a two lane road, and you could pick veggies and strawberries just about anywhere. We really enjoyed the rural atmosphere prevalent at that time. The only restaurant in town was Big Daddy's where we would take my mother to dinner when she visited from the north. We were very impressed with the Kings Point Clubhouse, which we thought was outstanding, and really sold us on the place. We spent many hours at the pleasant and so-clean Simmons Park in Ruskin, fishing and picnicking. We also enjoyed the many wonderful beaches.

We welcomed the many changes that took place over the years: the coming of South Bay Hospital; the new Community Hall; the Fitness Center; and more amenities than one can mention. Sun City Center is so beautiful, with its many lakes, golf courses, landscaping, and lovely homes. It's like a picture postcard. Best of all, we feel safe and secure.

Another bonus to Sun City Center is its proximity to Tampa, with its many attractions such as the Performing Arts Center, and Busch Gardens. One time we attended a show put on by dancers in Ybor City. We wore our Spanish outfits, and some people thought we were part of the entertainment. We got a kick out of that. As Phil was a former oarsman, we attended the crew races on Seddon Channel each year.
There are so many volunteers here—it's a community of people helping people. We all care about one another. We've had to call on the Emergency Squad several times ourselves. What a blessing to have those wonderful people available.

I would be remiss if I didn't mention the Good Samaritan Ball, which is the most elegant event of the year. We all dress up in our finest attire, and dance the evening away in the beautifully-decorated Kings Point Ballroom. We have attended this event for 17 consecutive years. The proceeds go to the Good Samaritan Fund which provides financial help for needy seniors.

After five years we sold our northern house, and had a house built near Community Hall, where we lived for twelve years. Then, beautiful Aston Gardens opened in 1999 and we moved there. We are still active, and enjoy life very much here, and hope to be able to do so for many more years.

CHEF DON

Tricia Smith

Executive Chef Donald Edge is a happy man. He has found his career home at the Golf and Racquet Club. After rising up through the ranks, getting to know every aspect of cooking, planning and managing first at the Hyatt and then at the Wyndham hotel in Tampa, five years in each, he came to the Club six years ago.

He was introduced at a Town Meeting by President of the West Central Region of WCI, Charlie Brasington, as the man who was going to turn the Club around. At first stunned by this announcement and with the idea that he had expected to have a customary stint of five years and then move on, he very soon found that he felt differently at the Club than he had ever felt before. When he had effected the necessary changes he had a staff that worked together as a team and members that became like family. That is not to say that it's an easy job. "There are so many ages, financial categories and culinary preferences it can be a real conundrum to satisfy everyone, " Chef Don says, " but it's very important to me that everyone be pleased." The membership in the Club was 1100 six years ago and is 3000 today.

Chef Don has two assistant chefs and his staff includes 14 cooks and four dishwashers. His training of the crew has been very thorough and they have great faith in him to make everything work out right. He took them on a tour to their main provider, Sysco, to learn grades and qualities of various foods. Beside the meals, lunch and dinner seven days a week at the club itself, they cater for the Ben Sutton Golf School, the Inn's preferred customers' breakfasts as well as private catering jobs as far away as Venice and Sarasota. Chef Don's eyes sparkle when he speaks about the Chef's Table which, of course, is his special monthly culinary creation and where he has most interaction with the diners. He spends a lot of his time on the computer, figuring costs, planning menus and allocation of personnel.

Long ago he learned that his career was hard on family life. He became divorced before he moved to Riverview where he lives now. His two daughters are with his ex-wife and he has his 11 year- old son with him. He has been so appreciative of the club members who have taken young Don to the movies or for other outings when he has been so busy. With it all he is a happy man and loves the challenges of Sun City Center.

Here She Is!
by Lee Trevino

I have always seen life as a "Great Adventure," and enjoyed life to its fullest. I, Leora N. Trevino, always referred to as Lee, entered the Ms. Senior Florida Pageant in January 1991, as just another adventure in my life. Mr. Hoffman, owner of Florida Design Communities, agreed to sponsor me and gave me permission to appear with the honorary title of Ms. Sr. Sun City Center, 1991.

The pageant was held at the Ruth Eckerd Hall in Clearwater, Florida. There were eight contestants, and we were judged on philosophy of life, interview with the judges, talent and evening gown competition. I tap-danced in a hobo costume with black lights. I was *so* surprised and excited when I won, and was crowned Ms. Senior Florida 1991. It was an adventure I'll never forget. I had so much fun!

I went on to compete in Atlantic City as a contestant in the Ms. Sr. America pageant in April of 1991. I didn't come in first, but won the coveted evening gown award.

I was recognized and honored wherever I went as an ambassador representing Ms. Senior America, Inc. throughout the state of Florida for the entire year of 1991. During my reign I tap-danced at numerous nursing homes, was presented, and danced, at the Florida State Fair, was introduced at a Florida Orchestra performance, and attended most of the model home openings and civic events held in Sun City Center at that time. My husband Eloy said he felt like he was "Driving Miss Daisy" to the many events we attended.

At one of the SCC model home openings it was advertised that Lee Trevino would be present, along with other celebrities. During this occasion a man arrived at the model home all excited. I greeted him at the door. He said, "I'm here to see Lee Trevino!" I said, "I'm Lee Trevino." He shouted, "No you're not! I drove 40 miles to see the golfer, Lee Trevino, and I want to see him." Needless to say, he went away very disappointed.

Since I was the first Honorary Ms. Sr. Sun City Center title holder to enter the Ms. Sr. Florida pageant, I, along with Joan Young, who was Ms. Sr. North Carolina 1988, decided to start a Seniors pageant here in SCC. We approached Janice Poindexter, at Freedom Plaza, to see if they would be our sponsor. They agreed, and she directed, with our help, the first pageant held in Sun City Center. It was a huge success, with Anne Becker being the first crowned Ms. Sr. Sun City Center 1992. I directed the pageants for the next five years, along with some excellent help. Our developer, Florida Design Communities, became our sponsors after that first year.

A LONG LOOK BACK
As told to Tricia Smith

"**I** came here as a dentist in 1963 and lived in Bradenton, said Dr. Gerry Isbell." "In Bradenton, " I interjected incredulously, Why didn't you buy one of those incredibly inexpensive houses in Sun City Center to live near your work?" "I was only 30 years old," he responded, coolly. They wouldn't let me."

In 1963 there were about one hundred houses built and the hub, at least for Dr. Isbell, was at the corner of 674 and 301. That's where he and Dr. Branner, the first medical men in Sun City Center, had their offices. There was a motel there, a restaurant and a little nine hole golf course. Those nine holes are in the area now known as St. Andrew's.

He became a part of the activities in Sun City Center and remembers vividly the day when the Sun City Center Rotary Club received its charter. It was the day Kennedy was shot. We were having coffee at Rachel's in Wimauma to talk about his memories of Sun City Center and he mentioned that he had been having breakfast at Rachel's at least 25 or 30 years. One person who goes back as far as he does is Mary Blanton, who was Post-mistress in those early days. She is now at Sun Trust Bank. Her husband was Del Webb's construction chief. "Everyone knows Mary," he assured me. Another of his old buddies is Max Cherboneaux, who was the original engineer of the project.

Dr. Isbell,, whose home was San Antonio, Texas, and his wife, were captivated by the new concept that Del Webb was promoting and took a trip to the Arizona Sun City. When the project manager of Sun City Center's location asked him to come here he and his wife were ready. They had met while he was in the Air Force in Maryland She had no interest in living in San Antonio but has loved living in Florida. He is still practicing dentistry as much as he wants, which gives him a lot of time to enjoy retirement and be able to cast a long look back at Sun City Center.

A Wonderful and Happy Retirement

Harold Corrigan

Formed many lasting friendships in 35 years as a Sun City Center resident. Friendships led to a wonderful social life.

Living in Sun City Center provided activities beyond belief with ballet at your doorstep.

The Emergency Squad and Security Patrol are plusses to life in Sun City Center. Having a wonderful and happy retirement.

Editorial comment: Harold speaks from long experience; He is ninety five years young.

Retiree Finds Another Career

Frank Thomas

My wife and I retired to Sun City Center in 1979 from Long Island, New York. We had chosen it after looking over a number of places in Florida.

Learning of my writing background, some of my neighbors suggested that I create a course that would help them to write about their lives, this to be passed on to their children and grandchildren.

Since this would take a good deal of my time and wasn't exactly what I had in mind, I decided to interview a cross section of community leaders. "Is there a real need for this?" I asked. They were unanimous in their encouragement. One pointed out that, since the family is the heartbeat of our society, any course that could help bring its members closer together was eminently worthwhile.

So, taking a lesson from the turtle, who never gets anywhere until it sticks its neck out, I, now close to Medicare age, stuck out mine. "What techniques out of my experience," I asked myself, "could I bring forth that would be helpful to adults from all walks of life and level of education?" For some people, writing can be intimidating. By the following year, 1980, I was ready to offer my course "Writing Your Personal Memoirs - A Family Gift."

I was hardly prepared for what followed once I took the course to the classroom. A single announcement in our local paper brought out 42 men and women who wanted to write about their lives for their families.

It went so well that soon I was asked to teach the course in three other adult centers including Elderhostel, and was being asked to make speeches on my subject before groups. I became so inspired by the warmth of these would-be memoirists that I became dedicated to teaching several thousand of them over the next 21 years. They are living proof that anyone can write his or her personal story, regardless of age.

Many have presented me with copies of their completed memoirs for my cherished collection with such titles as: "My Life Journey", "My Time was Different from Your Time", "Beyond my Wildest Dreams", and "The Laughter and Tears of Yesteryears."

After three years of teaching, I decided I wanted to share this idea and my techniques across the country. I spent the better part of a year writing a book manuscript and turned it over to an agent who recognized its merits. He did one multiple submission to nine publishers and it was enthusiastically accepted by Writer's Digest Books in Cincinnati. My book "How to Write the Story of Your Life" is still active today in bookstores and libraries. Thus far I have heard from readers in 46 states, Canada, England and Australia. Most thank me for writing the book and many have also sent me copies of their completed memoirs.

Call it luck, serendipity or what have you. This gratifying part of my life's journey happened in a special place, a friendly little retirement town run by volunteers, where people care, keep busy and yet always stop to say "hello." Thank you Sun City Center.

Dragged Kicking and Screaming into Paradise

Yvonne Ponsor

In 1992, my husband and I were living in Storrs, Connecticut, within a short distance of both of our children. I was an adjunct professor at Eastern Connecticut State University. I loved New England, I had a great job and a lot of friends. I had only one problem. My husband wanted to move to Florida.

Now I have always loved Florida. My father used to bring me down years ago when Florida was really Florida. But I did not want to leave the happy spot I had made for myself.

Well, you know what happened, of course. We came down for a trial run of a month, went home, and sold our house in two days! Since I was teaching, we had to wait until the end of the semester to leave, so we arrived in Sun City Center on June 2, 1993.

It was hot. I did not know anyone. I missed my children and my friends. I would never find another job I liked. I would never meet anyone or do anything or have any fun ever again. I knew that for a fact. On my early morning walks in those first weeks I often met up with a lovely man, my first friend. He had been here a couple of years and had had those same early misgivings, but he listened patiently to my whining.

"Give it time," he would say, "you will feel entirely different in a very short time."

Well, I guess it was about a month later that I was involved in the Writers' Club and working at the library as a volunteer. Within a short time, I found myself President of the Writers' Club and handling the used-book sales for the library. Soon I was appointed to chair the Library Committee. My husband and I were playing duplicate bridge twice a week and working out at the Fitness Center.

All this activity opened up vistas of friendship for me here in Sun City Center. Within a couple of years I could walk into a room full of people and know most of them, and call many as friends.

I believe that only in Sun City Center could this have happened. I believe that only in this community could one find so many strangers becoming friends.

The most astonishing thing about Sun City Center to me is that the opportunities for self-expression and involvement never dry up. There is always something new and interesting to do. There is always a new avenue for entrance into the community life. People have different tastes and interests, but I do believe that if you cannot find something to do here that is fulfilling, fun and engrossing, you are not trying very hard. The range of activities and opportunities here is almost limitless. Most of us find that there are not enough hours in the day nor days in the week to do all the things we would like to do. Prioritizing becomes crucial.

Nothing stops us. The people of Sun City Center are not only busy, they are indomitable. People come to the Fitness Center in wheel chairs, on walkers, with canes; they do not give up. They keep moving, meeting their friends for a chat and a smile, doing the best they can. I find this remarkable and admirable.

Last year I was asked to form a club for people who have some degree of impaired vision. We have about 50 members now, and all of them are active within the community, serving as members of the Lions Club, working in any area that allows them to demonstrate the fact that, while they may be handicapped, they are not disabled. They respond to challenge with courage and humor, and find ways to stay useful. Only here can you find that sort of caring and concern.

Perhaps the most unique asset in the community is one that I did not discover until I had been here for three years – the Community Church College. I became an instructor and was immediately impressed by the efficiency and variety, the scope of talent and devotion that I found. I was fortunate enough to be asked to come on board as the Academic Dean of the college in 1997, and I am still there - still having fun and still impressed. What fascinates me is that, each semester, we are able to come up with instructors, mostly residents, to teach such a range of subjects - arts, sciences, literature, languages, religion and all sorts of crafts, health, history - and to teach them so well.

Volunteers run the community, busy people who find the time to work with the Emergency Squad, the Security Patrol, hospital, Samaritan Services and, most generously of all, on the Community Association Board. All of these people are working tirelessly for the greater good of this splendid way of life we all enjoy here.

So - you can see that I have settled in here and am having a fine time. I miss my kids but I see them often. I miss the turning leaves of New England and the advantages of being close to New York City. I miss all that, but not all that much - I don't have time! I am too busy enjoying the sweet life here. This may not be absolutely, positively perfect in every way, but it is as close to heaven as I expect to get.

Taking the Leap

Judy Kramer

The first time I visited Sun City Center, I was 57 and on the cusp of what I thought was middle age. My husband, Oscar, was 60 and had just retired for the second time. Our youngest had graduated from college, the nest was empty, the dog had died, and my responsibilities for caring for my aging parents had recently ended when they died within weeks of each other. I joined Oscar in retirement.

After lots of reading, we decided to visit SCC for a look at retirement living. He immediately fell in love with what he saw and felt here. I loved what I saw but had very confused feelings about a number of things. It was difficult for me to imagine leaving our children and grandchildren, leaving the town I had lived in all my life, leaving old friends and trusted medical connections. And, in truth, when I looked at who lived in Sun City Center, I saw my parents. "I'm not there yet," I explained to Oscar. He said, somewhat wistfully, "You're just not 60 yet."

For these, and many other more personal reasons, we decided our retirements might have been premature and we both returned to new and exciting jobs.

Jump ahead three years. Retirement once again entices us and we visit Sun City Center for a second time. And what I see inspires me. I see people both younger and older than myself who are active, stretching themselves physically, intellectually and spiritually. I feel welcomed wherever I go (and there are many places to go!). We try everything we have time for, the gym, the pools, the clubs, religious services. We go our separate ways and talk late into the night about what we are feeling and seeing and doing. I relinquish the ghost of my parents' aging and begin to live in my own. I am ready to believe that lifelong relationships with my children and friends can continue to grow. I am comfortable here.

We begin to look at homes, refining our wants and needs with every place we visit. We find a lovely home and anguish about taking that leap. I can feel the fear in my belly as I let go of the trapeze I am used to, hang suspended in mid-air, and stretch to reach the trapeze that is swinging toward me. I grab Sun City Center and feel secure. We buy a home.

We, our children and friends, have mixed feelings about our moving almost a thousand miles away. Along with happiness, there is much sadness. We suddenly recognize the grieving process we will all go through. The goodbyes are long and hard. We pack up a home that has embraced us for 34 years, hug and kiss adult children who will continue to grow without us physically present in their lives daily, weekly, monthly. Cell phones become our lifelines. We sell our house and move into our new home.

Each day we are here we love it more. Our friends visit. Our children visit. And we grow in new directions. In this place we find wonderful friendships, interests, and talents we never knew we had.

But there is something special about living in Sun City Center, and I couldn't put my finger on it until I had a recent conversation with my daughter, Amy. She had just returned to the university that she had attended -- her first visit in ten years. "I didn't appreciate how wonderful it was back then to have all my friends living so close to me and to be able to get together whenever we wanted," she said. That's exactly how I feel about living here. I have the time. I have the friends. And I love what I'm doing. Perhaps Oscar was right. I'm 60 years old.

SERENDIPITY

Sally Hahn

Was it fate, or serendipity?

When I visited Sun City Center in 1996, just to get a bead on the place, Helen Neal of Coleman Connections showed me houses, the Fitness Center, the Golf and Racquet Club and many other attractions. She also showed me a catalog of the Community Church College that really excited me! None of the other retirement communities I'd looked at had anything like it.

When I retired the following spring, I headed right back to Sun City Center. While volunteering at the library, I met Virginia Feder, Registrar of the College. She asked me to assist her, which I did. Virginia saw her chance to pass the torch, and I became Registrar the next semester.

The excitement of coordinating the registration of more than 600 students in two days was incredible! In 2000, I was appointed Dean of the College, sharing that position with Yvonne Ponsor. Interestingly, Yvonne's class on Mythology was one that especially caught my eye when I first saw the College catalog. I still can't believe my good fortune in having a major role in the institution that played a major part in my decision to move here rather than to some other community in Florida.

A Banker / Sailor Moored to Sun City Center

Bill Hoskins

I first came to Sun City Center in 1981 at the tender age of 59 to assume the role of president of community-owned Sun City Center Bank. I had spent 20 years running a community bank in Libertyville, Illinois, had built two new bank buildings, and was getting a little bored. After talking with Sun City Center resident John Davies, a "shirt-tail relative" of my brother, and a member of the Board of Directors of the Sun City Center Bank about management problems at the bank, I thought, "Hey, what a neat idea it would be to slide on down to Florida where it's warm all year, wrestle with the bank's problems for a while, and slip into retirement in a climate that's a lot more fun than northern Illinois." One thing led to another and down I came.

Sun City Center Bank was a truly "community-owned bank," something of a rarity in these present days when banks have been absorbed into the "chain bank system," and was well regarded in the community. Its stock was widely spread through the area, with no one owning a really controlling interest in the bank. They were a fine board. Ellsworth Simmons, one of the founding directors of the bank, had been chairman of the Hillsborough County board, and he's the fellow whose name is on Simmons Park on Tampa Bay. Dentist Gerry Isbell, who still practices in Sun City Center, was on the Board, along with Chet Kendall who still lives in the Caloosa area. John Davies, my initial contact with the bank, (no longer with us) had been president of a bank in Wisconsin for many years before he became a full-time, long-time resident of Sun City Center. Board member Lou Ellen Wilson still serves an active and respected role in the community in the field of real estate management. Stan Whitcomb, another board member, is still active here in Sun City Center real estate development.

There was a very good spirit at the bank, and still is, evidenced by the fact that several of the people who worked at the bank in 1982 are still there. But the short history is that when the Bank Absorption Plague" (my name for it) swept through Florida and the rest of the nation starting in the early '80s, Sun Bank offered Sun City Center Bank's shareholders three times what the stock had been selling for, and it was well on its way to becoming a branch of the Sun Bank group (later melding into SunTrust).

Sun Bank's management offered me a senior vice presidency in Sun Bank, but I decided that my 23-year role as "Bank Head Honcho" probably made me unfit to function well in the lower echelons of management.

A lifetime devotion to sail boating lured me into a first two-year retirement to Longboat Key, and easy access to the sea aboard my 41-foot Morgan Out-Islander sailboat. I had moved out of Sun City Center partly because I felt a little too young for it.

I flunked retirement after a couple of years, and followed with a 3-year run as CEO of a bank in Schaumburg, Illinois, and a 3-year stint as CEO of a "start from scratch" bank just south of my Libertyville, Illinois starting ground, with final retirement at age 70. My wife, Jessie, and I then bought a 46-foot sailboat in Fort Lauderdale, put all our gear in a warehouse, and lived aboard for three years -- a wonderful adventure too long to recount here.

Sun City Center lured us back, and has been my cherished home since 1995. Jess died in '95, and I married her wonderful best friend, Pat, in '96, and here we are -- living happily ever after. And very much involved. Pat has been Pottery Club president, and now serves as a director for the Sun City Center Guardianship Foundation -- a wonderful institution. I have been involved with the Sun City Center News, the Community Church College, the Forum Club, the Sunset Dinner Dance Club, and now have as my central activity, bicycling with my buddy, Steve Csintyan, 25 to 50 miles a day after a breakfast at Rachel's in Wimauma. We travel country roads, squirting hostile dogs with my "Halt" spray, and cherishing the sunshine, the spider webs glistening with dew, the Sandhill cranes, the beautiful Florida sky and the cows and calves who stare at us as we pedal along, wondering what strange creatures we are.

My 20 Years with the Sun City Center Women's Chorus

John Phelps

In the fall of 1975, I was invited to direct the SCC Women's Chorus. It was an ideal situation because my wife, Dorothy, could be the accompanist. We cheerfully accepted.

My rehearsals always started with vocal warm-up exercises. There were two second sopranos who were inclined to be naughty, Lois Hill and Kay Lyon. They would intentionally sing wrong notes now and then. This always brought a laugh from the chorus and I had to pretend to be annoyed, but it relaxed the group and made the rehearsals fun.

Having Dorothy Phelps as my accompanist was a blessing. Not only did she play the piano beautifully, but she worked hard to have all of the accompaniments learned to perfection.

At concert times, Norma Hagner always lined up the ladies before going on stage. She was so efficient that I frequently called her "Sergeant Norma."

During the first year or two that I directed, a young lady by the name of Jennie Schimel sang with us. She was so young and energetic that we appointed her publicity chairman. At the time, Charlie's Angels was a popular television program. She decided that the chorus made such heavenly music, they should be called "Johnny's Angels." A former violin student of mine, Karen Reedy, volunteered to write suitable words, and so our Theme Song was born. We ended every concert by having all the ladies put on their halos and sing *Johnny's Angels* which ended with a chord held for a long time while I inspected "the troops" for askew halos. The audiences always loved this bit of humor. It was a sad moment for many when we sang for the last time.

Life, and the Big (Swing) Band

Kline Locher

When Fran and I arrived in Sun City Center from Orlando in 1986, we were pleased to find a welcome change from the hustle and bustle of "big city traffic."

Yes, we discovered a great lifestyle, including loads of amenities to please our many desires. But never for a moment did we foresee what the future held in store for us.

I had spent many years before retiring selling Hammond Organs and Steinway pianos. Since I was not an organist, I had to delve into my piano background and apply it in learning to play the organ so I could sell this product to my customers. From this background I became an "Organ hobbyist."

This led to a visit to the Kings Point clubhouse one day where I found an organ in the lobby being played by a slight blonde lady, Jean Little. As I watched her play, she asked if I played the organ. At her invitation I sat down and played .. and that is when it all started.

Shortly after this introduction, Jean Little died and I was asked to play a memorial tribute in her honor. From this beginning I was asked to play for the performers in the SCC Follies. This became a yearly event for me, one that I thoroughly enjoyed even though, at times, the many, many rehearsals and music changes almost drove me crazy.

As a result of the Follies, I started a small group called the Par 3 Band, consisting of an organ, drums and a male vocalist who had performed in the Follies. Unfortunately, after one of our holiday jobs, our vocalist suffered a stroke and died.

Enter my dear friend Norm Hinkley, a great jazz tenor saxophonist and vocalist. This was the start of the Par 3 Jazz Band. This group was augmented to become the Par 4 Jazz Band and performed successfully through the spring of 2000.

In 1991, Norm convinced me to join the Sun City Center Big Band as a piano player. During the intermission one night, the conversation got around to my musical background. When several band members discovered I had played lead trumpet for many of the great bands during the "Big Band Era" of the late 30's and early 40's, they suggested that I play trumpet in the Big Band instead of piano.

This could be a monumental task to get the horn out of mothballs and, after some 40 years, practice, practice, practice to regain a lost lip. The thought of playing again drove me to attempt what seemed to be an impossible task. I had originally planned to make a table lamp out of my horn but my wife would not tolerate the idea and, today, I'm very grateful that her decision was the right one. Finally, in 1992, I switched jobs from piano to trumpet.

Getting good arrangements for our band was difficult so, shortly after joining the trumpet section, I started to write some special charts for our band. Never in a million years would I have imagined that our playing library would consist of over 50% of my arrangements ten years later. I have now written over 300 arrangements for the Big Band, some good, some not so good. You never know how it will sound until it is actually played and rehearsed. When it is good, the 30+ hours it takes to write is well rewarded. BUT, when it is bad, the 30+ hours are like an eternity lost.

In 1992, Ed Forrest, the founder and leader of the Big Band, became ill and had to retire. The band members voted for me to become the new leader and that is where I hold forth today. By the spring of 2000, with the workload of leading the Big Band and arranging growing, I could no longer accept the responsibility of 2 bands and, therefore, the Par 4 Jazz Band was disbanded. All my concentration could then be focused toward the Big Band.

Although there have been many trials and tribulations in the band that I never expected after retiring from the business world -- such things as band members retiring, failure to perform due to illness, deaths ... all is forgotten when the curtain opens and the bright lights come on. The band plays and behold! The great sounds of the past are once again created. We are returned to the "Aura" of great music, good dancing and warm applause.

In 2002, due to some many out-of-town dates, we have changed part of the band's name. We believe the word "BIG" has no significance to most people, but the word "SWING" defines the character of the band. Therefore, we are now called the Sun City Center Swing Band.

Ah yes, this is a great time, a great place to live, warm friendships, and memories that will never fade. In Sun City Center we expect the best, never dreaming that the best was even better than what we had expected.

Being Needed in Sun City Center

by Phil Lange

Everything you'll ever need is already available in Sun City Center. Every interest already has its club. I considered myself a loner--a cautious, reluctant joiner. Yet, also by nature, and by employment, (teacher/professor) I've been a helping person, and in a helping profession. Where do I fit in?

Nature provided the entree. With unusual time, at first, to notice the birds and the squirrels outside the house, I began feeding them. Then, it was feeding the fish in the pond behind the house. Soon my attention was attracted to a "paper drive" that, every Saturday morning, had Sun City Center residents bring their newspapers to the collection point at the shopping center. During the years of its existence that paper drive produced over $300,000 for charity from its sale of re-cycled paper.

The birds, the squirrels, and the paper packers were regularly there, waiting. I was needed in the food chain! It was a small beginning in a complex community of interdependence and volunteerism.

Volunteerism is woven into the fabric of life in Sun City Center. We cannot escape awareness and appreciation of its great volume and range of specialized participation. Volunteerism takes on a personal dimension through the service by, or to, our friends and neighbors. And there are occasions when the dimension of longevity is added to that recognition.

Recently, for instance, while visiting a patient in South Bay Hospital, I encountered "Brownie," Emery Brown, wearing his "volunteer" attire.

"Brownie, it seems to me that you were here wearing a volunteer gown when this hospital first opened in 1982."

"Yes," he answered, "this is my 20th year as a volunteer here."

Volunteerism Brings Friendship and Fun

Rosie Clifton

When I first arrived in Sun City Center in October 2000, I was delighted to learn that there was an Indiana Club and they were about to have a party. I am proud to be from Indiana and enjoy being around Hoosiers. My husband, Ron, and I attended the party and had a very nice time at the potluck dinner. After dinner there was a short business meeting during which the president was trying to find a vice president. When the audience was asked for volunteers, my husband was the only one who raised his hand. I thought, "Gee, that's nice; Ron is going to help them out and be vice president." When he was recognized by the president Ron said, "My wife will do it; she will be your vice president!" So that was my start of volunteerism in Sun City Center!

Planning and having parties is the main business of the Indiana Club. During this process I have met many wonderful people who, while they won't serve as officers, readily volunteer to help plan the parties. I have made many friends from this group, and my best friend in Sun City Center was the first person to greet me at the Indiana Club.

Three months later, after having moved into and decorated my house, I saw a notice in the Sun asking for volunteers for FunFest 2001. I had no idea what FunFest was but it had 'fun' in the title so I volunteered. I joined the Communications and Publicity Committee. For a brief time I thought that, by default, I was going to have to be chairman but was quite relieved to find out that the leadership was to be by John Bowker. He was a very capable leader so I felt quite comfortable in assuming the role of recruiting and training the greeters at FunFest 2001. Once again, through the committee meetings and greeter contact, I met some wonderful people who have become friends.

Unfortunately, at one point I became sick and had a very difficult six-week recovery. I could not believe the outpouring of love, prayers, support, concern, cards, gifts, visits and help we received. (Because my husband is recovering from a stroke, his help was limited to cheering me up and checking on me.) My new friends rallied around us and helped more than I could ever believe. Various people shopped for us, took us to doctors' appointments, cooked for us, washed clothes, and helped in many ways. (When I arrived in town I joined a sorority and they were very, very helpful also.) One friend even spoon-fed me in bed when I was too weak to leave the bed. All in all, it brings tears to my eyes every time I think of the help I received from people I had not known a year before! Almost all of the people who helped were people I had met while volunteering.

Recently I was asked to be Co-President of the Woman's Club, one of the oldest clubs in Sun City Center, and a very active club. The reason they asked me, I am reasonably sure, is that they know I am a volunteer and that I have not "fallen on my sword" too often in my various projects. Besides, I don't think they could persuade anyone else to be president. In my opinion, those who declined could be making a mistake. I figure, I may not be a great president, but I know I will make lots of friends and have a lot of fun!

Expatriates Retire in Sun City Center

Dr. Dallas Tuthill

Expatriates? Yes, after many years in the medical profession in the United States, Dallas Tuthill and wife Norma lived and worked in Saudi Arabia for six years, until they retired and moved to Sun City Center in 1990.

Before giving up workin' for a livin' Dallas, physician, and Norma, medical secretary, decided in the "80's" to try an exotic environment overseas. Both went on work visas to Saudi Arabia, which was essentially the only way for non-citizens to enter. No tourism for outsiders - in those days anyway.

Norma, never having lived overseas, was skeptical, especially about going to the Middle East. "We'll be living in the desert in a tent, I suppose," she said apprehensively. Dallas, having served for more than a couple of decades in the U.S. Army (*retired in 1977*), had been posted around the world, including Viet Nam. He felt only eager anticipation: *One last overseas adventure!*

They worked in a hospital on a Saudi military base in Tabuk for a year, and then for five more with ARAMCO in an excellent 350-bed American-style hospital in Dhahran, in the Persian Gulf.

They came to know some of the many expatriate Americans who live most of their lives in foreign countries: An intelligent, enterprising, interesting group for the most part. One of the colleagues at the hospital was a second-generation ARAMCO expatriate, and his children were growing up there as well.

An adventure it was, indeed! They worked hard; toured all over Saudi Arabia; made their own wine, camped out many times on the Red Sea and in the desert, got to know and respect the Arabs, including the Bedouins and their history, became skeptical of the ruling royal family, toured extensively in North Africa, Southeast Asia; made some money - *and missed the biggest adventure of all, the Gulf War*! They started home in March 1990.

So how did they pick Sun City Center? Well, one of their expatriate bridge friends had invited her parents to visit. Where'd those parents come from? You guessed it. Of the retirement town they couldn't have been more laudatory: "You *must* see Sun City Center!"

Veni, vidi and was "vici'd."

In addition to bridge, golf and tennis hobbies, Dallas and Norma soon got into volunteer work. Dallas had often talked in the bowels of hospitals around the world about volunteer work, but was never involved to any degree. For him it started with the Men's Club of Sun City Center, and he and Norma soon were on the Security Patrol. She also has volunteered with the SCC Library and the Woman's Club. Dallas was privileged to work his way up to the presidency of the Men's Club in 1994 and 5 and, after being a Captain for some seven years, capped Patrol work as a director on the Security Patrol Board. For almost eight years he wrote a monthly prostate cancer newsletter, and facilitated the Sun City Center Prostate Cancer Education and Support Group ("Man to Man"). And he served for a time on the board of the American Cancer Society in Brandon.

Also in 1998, with the essential help of others - especially Kenneth Albrecht of Kings Point - he started a series of annual "educational seminars" staged at Sun City Center. Most seminars featured panels of medical experts, but one consisted of a judge and several lawyers. Each of these seminars attracted between 300 and 500 attendees.

But for Dallas, the piece de resistance has been the Community Foundation of Greater Sun City Center. From 1996 to term limits in June 2002, he was privileged to serve (last four years as chairman) on the Advisory Council of this foundation, an outreach satellite of the Community Foundation of Tampa Bay. The Foundation's mission is to enhance the quality of life for all residents of South Hillsborough County.

The local foundation will always be a work-in-progress, and it has earned the respect of many South Hillsborough County community leaders. By 2002, the foundation's asset base had grown to about $14 million and, from July 2001 to June 2002, more than $300,000 was granted from "undesignated" donor-advised and field-of-interest endowment funds. And in the same year, much more was distributed from "designated" endowment funds.

Now mostly re-retired, Dallas and Norma cherish the good memories that a full life in Sun City Center has made possible. They intend "to stay and play" in this wonderful town until carried out "feet first."

Community Volunteering

by Carla Miles

We traveled the country looking for a place to retire. We actually picked out a house in Sun City West in Arizona. On the way home to Minnesota, my husband Lee said he couldn't wait to get back to green grass. I said - "you don't want to live in Arizona!"

I ordered the video for Sun City Center, Florida, and we came down and checked it out. We purchased a home on the very lot that I had picked out on the map previous to our visit to Florida. We hadn't actually considered Florida before we saw the video. We had only traveled with our motorhome to the south and west.

We enjoyed living in Sun City Center. Lee was in such varied activities as Pelican Players, writers' groups, the C.A. Board and volleyball. He was also active in the United Community Church and enjoyed taking classes at the Community Church College.

Tony Shuen asked me to mention the volunteer project I created in Wimauma in 1995. It is now a 501-C-3 organization and we have a 12-member board. The project, called the Hope Fund, provides scholarships for children in the after-school and summer programs at Bethune Park. We have a Boys and Girls Club in place and we hope to have summer swimming programs for the children. The Hope Fund has also raised funds for computers, exercise equipment for teens, a fifteen-passenger van, a mentor program and a tutoring program and anything else that we feel will enhance the program for the children and teens. We have plans for a shelter that will extend the physical space for the children.

Lee was very supportive of me and my project.

Sun City Center fulfilled our retirement.

We Love Sun City Center

Ruth & Bob Saxon

It has been said, "If you live in Sun City Center for three years, you'll be disappointed when you get to heaven."

That saying may be a little exaggerated, but having lived in Sun City Center for fourteen years, we couldn't think of a better place to live in retirement. We purchased a home in the Wedgewood Section in 1988 and lived there happily for nine years before moving a mile down the street to Independent Living at Aston CourtYards where we have lived for five years. The great thing in Sun City Center is that, as you get older, you can move from Independent Living to Assisted Living and then to Dependent Living ... all within the borders of Sun City Center, keeping the same friends, church, etc., etc.

Our community has been built and thrives because of our resident *volunteerism.* As an example, Ruth and I served on the Security Patrol team for twelve years. (Our Security Patrol has been credited for the lowest crime rate in Hillsborough County.) We both have been active in our church and, for nine years, headed the Share Food Program in this area.

Bob has been a Lion for thirty-three years, fourteen in Sun City Center. During his term as president, the Lions, Kiwanis and Rotary Clubs sponsored a community picnic on Memorial Day to honor the widows and widowers of deceased veterans. Also during his term, the Service Clubs, Veterans organizations and the Chamber of Commerce sponsored the flying of American flags on State Route 674 on special American holidays. Bob has also volunteered at South Bay Hospital and both of us continue to volunteer for different organizations in Sun City Center.

Lastly, for a small yearly fee, one can belong to any of over 100 clubs for enjoyment and to learn new skills and make new friends. **We LOVE Sun City Center**!

Joy of Living in Sun City Center

Dolores Berens

My first impression of Sun City Center was the day before closing on our house in May 1987. The Unit 47 Property Owners Association was having their yearly block party. My husband and I were invited to attend as new home owners in the Association. Everyone was so friendly and interested in knowing about us. It was a wonderful feeling for us new people moving into a completely new town and state with only one friend in town.

Being a sewer, I was thrilled to see the Sewing Club room and quickly joined. Also, I quickly joined a Bowling League as that was my one great passion up north.

I joined the Woman's Club and became very active in all their philanthropic projects; recently completing my second two-year term as president.

As I had worked since the age of 16 (all of my life) it was difficult to adjust to not working when I came to Florida. So, I went to work for the Cypress Creek Development for a year and a half. I was then able to join the American Business Women's Association in 1989, served as its president, and was named Woman of the Year in 1994.

Being involved in many programs and clubs in Sun City Center, and very interested in the government of the town, I was asked to serve as a Director on the Community Association Board. I served for 2-1/2 years. It was great getting to know the people. After finishing my term, I joined the Samaritan Alzheimers Auxiliary and became its president 3-1/2 years ago. This is the Respite Group in the Greater Sun City Center area and is a program close to my heart. My sister-in-law, cousin and aunt all have had Alzheimers. This is a job that needs to be done in our area.

I would never move to any other location in my lifetime! My feeling is you never have to look anywhere else for something to keep yourself busy and happy. You just have to reach out and someone is there for you. Sun City Center, Florida is the easiest place to make friends. Our town is so beautiful - the services for the needy are excellent. There is a life style for everyone.

I love this town!!

Thanksgiving in Sun City Center

by Kathryn M. Beers

Over the river and through the woods
To Grandmother's house we'll go.
What a beautiful thought, but I must confess
We had no sleigh nor a flake of snow.

Was I feeling sad
And saying, "What a pity!"
Because our folks up North
Spend Thanksgiving in Sun City.

In place of a sleigh,
Grandpa used his golfcart.
With many hands on the wheel,
They all felt quite smart.

Not all bundled up
To play in the snow,
But in bright-colored swimsuits
To the pool they did go.

While Grandpa entertained
And they were all having fun,
I was testing the turkey
To see if it was done.

The table was set
With my best China dishes
As my heart overflowed
With thanks and good wishes.

There was noise and loud laughter
As they all came rushing in,
With sun-burned foreheads,
Noses and chins.

They knew before dinner
There were things they must do.
You can bet they were ready
In just a minute or two.

As we all gathered round
Both the young and the old,
There was one thing certain,
'Twas a sight to behold.

Before partaking
Of the turkey and dressing,
We all bowed our heads
While Grandpa asked God's blessing.

There was singing and laughter,
Not a frown or a fret,
For it was a special Thanksgiving
One we'll never forget

Kathryn M. Beers

Time and Beauty

by Kathryn M. Beers

A year, a day, a moment, all pass so quickly;
Proving the old adage, "Time waits for no man."
So it's wise to live each day to the fullest,
Enjoying life the very best that you can.

Time! Time awards me a daily stroll.
I walk rather slowly, for I'm not in a race
The warmth of the sun, and the scent of fresh air
Put a smile on my old and wrinkled face.

I'm surrounded by nature, its sights and its sounds,
There's a woodpecker boring a little round hole,
Never pausing a moment, just pecking away,
Making himself a home, that telephone pole.

Just a stone's throw away is a grand old oak,
Dropping its acorns and littering the ground.
A bushy-tailed squirrel is enjoying the treat,
As it nibbles and nibbles and scampers around.

By a red flowering bush stands a snowy white egret,
Not a feather moving, it's perfectly still.
It must see something with those small slanty eyes.
Snap! Up with a salamander clutched tight in his bill.

Now down by the lake with its lilies in bloom,
Is a mother duck and her ducklings gracefully paddling away.
At my foot a huge turtle snuggles tight in its shell.
It will poke out its head later on in the day.

Dark clouds are gathering and hiding the sun.
I'll head for home before rain drops fall.
For these sights of Sun City, a thank you to God,
Who created this beauty to be enjoyed by all.

Oh! Sun City Center
by Tony Shuen

Oh! Sun City Center, Oh Sun City Center,
A place in the sun,
A community where living is fun,
My love for thee has just begun.

No more Monday morning blue,
No more icy roads and shoveling snow.
No more interferences with favor
In games and hobbies we actively pursue
In harmony and friendship together,
We live happily ever after.

Over the years we've grown a little rounder,
But with each pound we gained,
There is more to give to one another.
As time goes by we are all getting maturer,
But with every wrinkle that shows,
We are kinder and wiser than ever.

And where in the world can one find no matter
In spring, summer, fall or winter.
Palms are swaying,
Flowers are blooming,
Birds are singing,
Fish are jumping, and
One's spirit soaring.

If there is a Paradise on Earth,
Believe you me, my friends,
Sun City Center is the nicest place of all.

Sun City Center--a Great Place to Live
by Edith Long

Sun City Center, a great place to live,
You better believe it, thousands sure did.
There is golf and tennis and lawn bowling, too,
Shuffleboard courts just to mention a few.
Every kind of craft will sure keep you busy,
And all of the bridge games would make you plain dizzy.
Want to go for a swim and exercise, too?
Outdoors or in, there is a pool for you.
A great band to dance to, and dancers galore,
Whether it's line-dance or square, they are out on the floor.
There are many great things for you provided,
And your health and welfare haven't been slighted.
Emergency Squad, and Good Samaritans are there
When help is needed they do more than their share.
But best of all are the people you meet,
Just strolling along our wonderful streets.
Whichever part of the town you choose,
Each has its benefits--you just can't lose!
This town isn't made of just mortar and brick,
It's you and you that make Sun City Center click

Getting Older With Wit and Wisdom in S.C.C.

by Max Slater, M.D.

Longevity is the result of heredity and environment, nature and nurture. We can not change facts, but we can change attitude, which affects longevity. We can not change genes, but we can change the environment.

It is an established fact that tobacco, excessive alcohol and forbidden drugs are deleterious to health. However, there are conflicting opinions about carbohydrates, fats, proteins, cholesterol, salt, and certain additives. But there is no doubt about the effects of obesity on longevity. This cannot be emphasized enough. Count calories, not cholesterol. There is the additional fact that ice cream, chocolate, cake and pie make one feel good—which stimulates good hormones and aids longevity.

I have, for many years, collected one-liners which deal with old age. A few are original. Nearly all have been modified to stress a point. Here they are:

- The trick is to get older, but not old.
- Do not stop exercise and sports because you are getting older. You will get older when you stop.
- No eyes, no muscles, no reflexes, no wind. It is remarkable how well you can do without these.
- I feel like a young man with a few things wrong with my muscles and joints.
- Do the best you can with what you have left.
- The older I get, the longer everyone else is off the tee.
- Since I have become older I find that my golf swing is as good as ever, but the difference is that I walk more slowly to my ball, and get there faster.
- Since I have become older I have difficulty deciding whether a putt is downhill or uphill. I solved this by walking from the ball to the hole. If I get out of breath, I know it is uphill. If I stumble, I know it is downhill.
- Life is like riding a bicycle—you fall off when you stop pedaling.
- When you get out of breath tying your shoelaces, or eating grapefruit, it is time to give up tennis.
- One of the joys of old age is that of not going.
- The trick is to die young as late as possible.
- Old age is that period of life when more and more things happen for the last time, and fewer things happen for the first time.
- How old would you be if you did not know how old you were?
- Youth is a gift of nature, old age is a work of art.
- All the great and good men of this world are either dead or dying, and I am beginning to feel not so well myself.
- Never stop living for fear of dying.

My Fifteen Minutes
by Bob Larson

Remember the pop artist Andy Warhol who painted pictures of cans of Campbell tomato soup? He once said that everyone experiences 15 minutes of fame sometime during his or her life. Does being included in an article in a national newspaper count?

One evening in October, 1999 the phone rang. I answered it trying to be less snarly than usual when anticipating another telemarketer call.

"Hello."

"Is this Mr. Larson:"

"Yes it is."

Obviously having suffered rejection when calling a stranger he got right to the point. "I'm Thomas Fogarty from Arlington, Virginia. I write for USA Today. You live in Delray Beach, don't you?"

"No! You definitely have the wrong number. I live in Sun City Center."

"Oh good, that's a retirement community. Do you own your own home?"

Sensing a scam, I hesitated briefly, but curiosity got the better of me. I definitely wasn't going to give him my social security or credit card number. "Yes I do, but you have the wrong Larson."

He surprised me by responding, "It seems like I have the wrong person, but I'd still like to interview you about community living if you don't mind. Did you pay cash for your home?"

"Yes, we did."

"This is great," he said. "Did you know that Sun City Center has a higher percentage of cash sales than any other retirement community in the United States?"

Now my interest was really piqued.

Forty five minutes later Tom said, "Thanks, Bob, for the interview. You've been extremely helpful. If you don't mind, I'll send over a photographer to take a few pictures within the next couple of days. The article should appear in USA Today next week."

If this caller was a scammer, he was good. We were even on a first name basis.

The next day we received a call from a professional photographer. "This is Robert Rogers. I'd like to come out to your place to take some pictures for USA Today."

Mr. Rogers took approximately 50 pictures of us in almost every position except standing on our heads.

Sure enough, the article appeared on the front page of the Money section of the November 1, 1999 issue of USA Today. Our picture appeared across the top of the article. Small pictures of two other people were contained in the article--General Alexander Haig and Oprah Winfrey. General Haig and his wife paid $4.9-million cash for an eight and a half bath home in Palm Beach, Florida. Oprah Winfrey didn't need a mortgage to buy a $600,000 condo in Fisher Island, Florida.

Is it possible that our pictures are included in Alexander's and Oprah's scrapbooks?

Several weeks after the article appeared we received a copy from friends who spotted it in a USA Today while visiting in Brussels, Belgium. Some other friends discovered it in the paper while waiting in the Denver airport.

We were famous--for about 15 minutes.

The Kings Point Navy

by Howard H. Marx

It was in 1983 when we moved into our new home located in the Gloucester section of Kings Point.

I had been looking forward to playing the Cypress Greens Golf Course for a long time, and now I was finally ready to play. At that time there was no club house, and only nine holes of golf.

At long last the starter announced that it was time for our foursome to tee off. We negotiated the first two holes and were enjoying the course and the excitement of playing it for the first time. The third hole started off innocently enough, but as I prepared to hit the second shot I saw out of the corner of my eye that the parked golf cart was slowly starting to move down the gentle slope toward the lake with nobody in the cart!

I ran toward the cart, hoping to jump in and prevent it from going into the lake. However, it had picked up speed and I was unable to catch up to it. Much to my chagrin I watched helplessly as the cart ran into the lake and buried its front end in the mud.

Our foursome tugged and pulled, but we were unable to budge the cart. How humiliating it was to realize that I had not set the brake on the unattended cart.

Fortunately, a road-building crew was nearby and the kind and friendly operator of the road-grader retrieved the cart. No serious damage was done to the golf cart, but my ego was badly damaged!

For many months after this incident I was known as Howie Marx, Admiral of the Kings Point Navy.

Old Model T's Never Die

by Norma Powers

Something new appeared on the scene in Sun City Center, Florida, in January, 2002, when my husband Fred and I moved from Punta Gorda, where we had spent 27 years, to our new home at Freedom Plaza. That something new was a Model T Ford.

Fred's career had been with Eastman Kodak, working on the Manhattan Project in Oakridge, Tennessee where work moved forward on development of the atomic bomb, followed by assignments in Manila for four years, and Singapore for twelve.

A void occurred in our lives, in Singapore, when daughter Penny left to attend Michigan State University. We decided we needed a new interest to fill this void, and remembered, of all things, the Model T Fords we had seen in Australia during a trip there. Model T's were plentiful there—still used by farmers in the Outback.

With help from the Kodak manager in Canberra we were able to obtain a handsome 1926 Model T roadster which he had crated, and shipped to Singapore in late 1965. It arrived in good shape, and Fred was able to drive it right out of the packing crate. He found an elderly Chinese gentleman who was quite well informed about Model T's, who maintained it for the duration of our stay in Singapore.

In 2000, while we were making plans to move to Sun City Center, Paul Beitler, the husband of daughter Penny decided to have the Model T restored as a surprise for his in-laws. He had it sent by truck to Canada, the land of its birth, where it was completely restored with a beautiful dark maroon body—an authentic original color—and black fenders. When finished, the Model T was again trucked back to Sun City Center, and delivered to Fred and me in time for Thanksgiving that year. The whole family was here to celebrate.

"Elizabeth," as Fred called his car—not Tin Lizzie—has brought pleasure to many in Sun City Center. Two men have been especially helpful keeping "Elizabeth" in shape, and taking it for rides—Jack Allender of Ruskin, and Mr. "Sonny" Pruitt of the

Transportation Department at Freedom Plaza. Pruitt has told some of the folks at Freedom Plaza, "It's the most beautiful thing I ever saw. It took my breath away."

The cherished Model T has had a distinguished career. Elizabeth won the Singapore Grand Prix three years in a row. Son-in-law Paul Beitler and son Justin flew in from Chicago to drive the precious car in SCCs 30th anniversary parade.

This fabulous Model T, which once helped fill a void in the lives of Fred and me has now become part of the Beitler family, Paul and Penny, and their children JP, Justin and Jessica, in keeping with our wishes after Fred passed away on March 20, 2002. Elizabeth will be housed at the Beitler's vacation home in Boca Grande, Florida.

Old Model T's never die—they just become loved by new families.

Early Volleyball Club
by Charles Clapp

When my wife and I retired to Sun City Center in 1970 one of the first couples we met was Irving and Dorothy Reynolds. Irving, who had been a volleyball coach in high school, and was a keen promoter of the game, had organized the Volleyball Club a few years earlier. I was happy to join in the fun. The games were played on a grass court laid out on the lawn extending westward from the entrance to the old Town Hall. The net was set up parallel to Cherry Hills Drive between two of the three large oak trees still standing there. Of course, those trees were much smaller thirty years ago. The wooden bench around the base of one tree was enjoyed by spectators and resting players alike.

At that time the club membership was not much greater than the twelve needed to fill our one court. Playing skills were about at the level you would expect to find at a family picnic. Only two or three members were tall enough, or had enough spring in their legs, to be able to reach above the net, while the rest of us played an earth-bound game. "Coach" Reynolds would occasionally halt play to demonstrate a correct playing technique, a task that must have strained his patience to the limit, but, gentleman that he was, he never allowed it to show. Even without benefit of effective "spiking" or "blocking" we still had a challenging game that provided healthful exercise and amiable comradeship, and the continued growth in membership attested to the Club's popularity.

The two trees flanking the court were a shadowy but undeniable presence in the games. I remember several occasions when the ball found a resting place in the branches of one of them, and just sat there, daring us to dislodge it. Sometimes, in a fit of madness, we would try to knock it down with our spare ball, whereupon—you guessed it—we then had two balls up a tree instead of one. Eventually we would find a long pole, or some other means, to break the impasse and continue the game.

Eventually it became impossible to maintain the grass surface against our bi-weekly activities and the Community Association found the money to build us a hard-surface court just to the north of the Lapidary clubroom. We found the new court much to our liking though the surface was less friendly than grass in the event of a fall, or when a spirited player dove to retrieve a low ball. And though the ball could no longer hide from us in a tree, it could now hop over the fence and cause pandemonium in a game on the adjacent lawn bowling green.

As our membership grew, a second hard-surface court was added next to the first. And, with time, the club went through other changes. Coach Reynolds retired from the club for health reasons about twenty years ago, more new members arrived who, having grown up with volleyball, were able and eager to play the game at a higher level of skill. For physical reasons I decided to quit the game about fifteen years ago. So I cannot say anything about the Club as it moves to its new courts near the new Community Hall. However, I hope they develop as many fond memories of their activities there as I have of the early years of the Volleyball Club.

Tennis at the Golf & Racquet Club

by Luisa Reagan

Many of my happy days spent in Sun City Center were on the tennis court.

We played evenly matched games on the well-maintained Hard-Tru surface. It's a synthetic material that makes you feel as if you are playing on a clay court, since it is easier on your legs and feet. The surface lets you slide to reach the ball, charge the net, and run for the drop shots. The balls also tend to bounce a little slower, and you rally for a longer period.

We often cheered our opponent's good shot. One observer questioned why we cheered our opponents when we lost the point. We replied that we simply respect our opponents, and a good shot, no matter who made it.

It was fun to hear one of our players call out the score, "fifteen all, y'all." The Ladies' Round Robin and Lunch added to the social atmosphere. Sunday mixed-double games have been played for over twelve years. We played from 8 AM to 9:30 AM, starting when the sun got warm and the breezes were gentle. They were friendly games. The air was filled with camaraderie, excitement and laughter. We indulged in fun first, and church later.

The best part came after the game. We would retreat to court-side where tables and chairs were set up under umbrellas and trees. Fresh-brewed coffee was provided by the tennis pro, Tom Rose. We would rotate bringing doughnuts or other pastries. Occasionally we would have toasted bagels, cream cheese and lox—a special treat.

When one of our players, Gary Geers, collapsed on the court, one day, we were fortunate to have Dr. Ron Peets playing. Ron used mouth-to-mouth resuscitation to revive Gary, no doubt saving his life. After five months Gary was back on the court.

At times we needed a substitute. One regular was Norman Winter, who was in his nineties, a perfect gentleman who plays a skillful game of tennis.

As avid tennis players, we always looked for the opportunity to play tennis on holidays. On St. Patrick's Day "Pro" Tom Rose would cook his favorite corned beef and cabbage. Rain or shine, we gathered under a big tent.

For Valentines Day the ladies were presented with candy and corsages. What a sight on the green courts! Thanksgiving Day included "The Turkey-Shoot." Each one would serve three times. The one who hit the target on the other side of the net won "the turkey." The "Christmas Hot-Dog Roast" was a tradition.

Those were happy days—truly memorable and unforgettable.

Lawn Bowling, a Way of Life
by Larry Hanley

I decided to take early retirement in 1975. One day as I was walking through the County Park in Bloomfield, New Jersey, I came upon a group of people lawn bowling. When they invited me to join them and try my skills, I became very interested. My wife Grace also liked the game, and we both bowled regularly. After a couple of years we thought it would be nice to move to Florida where we could bowl year 'round.

In our travels in Florida we came upon Sun City Center. In Sun City lawn bowling got to be a way of life. I always said the only people we know well are my neighbors and other lawn bowlers.

Bowling in Sun City Center we met bowlers from all over the United States and foreign countries. Our SCC team traveled to other parts of the country to meet and compete against other teams, and they would come to visit us here. In a few instances we hosted international matches in Sun City Center.

A number of years ago I was invited to a meeting called by Sun City Center's developer. He wanted suggestions and ideas to be used in advertising. At this meeting a nice little lady said, "When I die and go to heaven, I hope it is just like Sun City Center." That sounds pretty good to me, too.

Sawdust Engineers

by Bernard DeLeo

Sawdust Engineers is one of the oldest clubs in Sun City Center. Shortly after Del Webb started Sun City Center in 1962 he set aside a place where residents could come and do woodworking for home repairs, or other projects. Over the years a lot of SCC residents have spent many hours making things for themselves, but, more so, making things for others.

In 1984 the Engineers became a non-profit corporation and directed much of their efforts toward making items for children. They have maintained a large inventory of educational items, toys and games. These items are available to teachers who may receive up to seven items per year without charge. This helps provide items that teachers would not otherwise be able to afford. Last year, 547 items were distributed. The most popular item is a dollhouse with 24 pieces of furniture.

Sawdust Engineers also provides many items for the community. They have made most of the wooden benches for Lowry Park Zoo, and picnic tables for Hillsborough County Nature classes. They have recently made 36 foot-lockers for the Tampa Bay Childrens' Home so that each child his or her own locker.

The group constructed the model of the proposed new facilities for Sun City Center, and that model has been on display in the SCC Atrium.

Many residents come in with small requests such as cutting a board, and receive a friendly response and help from Engineers. The workers make wheel chair ramps, where a need is found, at no cost. However, donations are always welcome. Last year there were 80 special requests for which they made 4,180 pieces. They are not into the business of constructing buildings, but they can make almost any item of wood.

The Sawdust Engineers' shop is next door to the Lap Pool, along the walkway to the outdoor pool. The shop is open from 8 AM to 4 PM Monday through Saturday. Membership is open to any member of the Sun City Center Community Association.

Sun City Center Woodcarvers

by Bill Potter

Back in the early 1990s a nucleus of the present day Carvers was formed at the United Community Church College by instructor Jim Morris. During that time other SCC residents were carving at the Presbyterian Church in Bradenton. During 1993 the various carvers were coming together and meeting in one of the lobby rooms of the Town Center building. By the end of 1993 there were eleven active members who applied to the SCC Community Association for formal club recognition. The present day Woodcarvers Club started in January, 1994, meeting in the Swan Room under the presidency of Eleonore Madigan. The Club currently boasts a membership of 50, and meets in Room 3 of the Community Hall.

From the inception of the Club, the woodcarvers have, by necessity, met only one morning per week because of the limited facilities allocated to them. With the steady increase of interest for woodcarving within the community, and with the increase of talented and experienced wood carvers moving into Sun City Center, the members are now looking forward to moving into a full-time-use club room currently under design, and to be located adjacent to the Sawdust Engineers work shop.

In 1996 I moved to Sun City Center and joined the Club. I had been carving for 18 years, had attended three semesters of carving training under Master Carver Peter Newton at St. Petersburg Junior College. I was president of the Calusa Woodcarving Club in New Port Richey. This club had formal training patterned after the classes I took at the college. I brought this knowledge to Sun City Center and soon began teaching, and was elected president of the Club. Classes contained up to ten students, and approximately forty carvers have taken the classes while the club membership grew to fifty. I have tried to teach the classic way of carving including how to use the tools, the effect of grain and transition points, how to slice instead of push, care of tools, and sharpening, etc.

There was as much socializing as there was carving, and kidding and story-telling ran rampant. Most new carvers were sure they would never become good sculptors, but many soon moved up alongside experienced carvers.

In 1996, Art Nyberg, an award-winning bird carver from the Boston, Mass. area, joined our club and immediately started teaching bird carving. He is adept at teaching bird anatomy, feathering and painting.

Caricature carving is popular, and generally involves whimsical or comical animals and people.

The annual SCC FunFest is an event where Woodcarvers exhibit our works, and display the ribbons and awards won at the Florida State Fair and other shows. This year we filled a big room with our handiwork, including "The Full Moon Saloon," carved by Jack Bernard, which always draws a crowd as its carver/bartender, always eager to shoot the breeze about the free beer and easy women in his saloon, explains his masterwork. Over 200 wood carvings were displayed at the last FunFest.

SCC Woodcarvers Club members won a total of 13 ribbons at Florida State Fair 2001. Carvers work on these carvings for a year or more to get them ready to compete with other Florida carvers.

At the church's request, club members carved a cross of Celtic design for St. Andrew Presbyterian Church. The cross stands 50 inches high and took six months to complete. It was made of oak and was carved with intricate design. It was gifted to the church and now hangs on a wall of the chapel.

WANT TO PLAY BRIDGE?
By Mary Rutledge

The Sun City Center Bridge Club, hereafter referred to as the Club, obtained a franchise and began playing duplicate bridge under the ACBL (American Contract Bridge League) in 1963. At that time the Club held one game a week at the Community Hall and had seven or eight tables. To date the Club has grown to over 400 members. Our membership contains all levels of skills, from beginners/novice to players who have 5000 points and are Life Masters. Our games are held in the Horizon and Caper rooms. The Horizon room, where most of the games are held, is equipped with oversized bridge tables. Handicap chairs for those who need them, bidding boxes, water fountains, book shelves, bridge books and pocket books that have been donated for the convenience of our bridge players. Coffee is served at most games. Bridge is played in Sun City Center daily.

The Sun City Center Bridge Association holds regular games on Monday evenings, Tuesday, Wednesday, Friday and Saturdays. On Friday afternoon there is also a novice duplicate bridge game, on Saturday afternoon a 199er game, meaning no one can play in that game if they have 200 or more points. During the months of November, December, January, February and March there is a Bridge + game on Tuesday evenings. At this game there is a brief instruction and then bridge play, with help from the teacher/ director.

These games are in addition to our regular games, all of which are stratified. All of the Directors of the games are ACBL certified. This is also true of our bridge teachers. If you haven't had enough bridge so far, there are Duplicate Bridge games played at King's Point on Tuesday and Thursday nights and Monday afternoon. There are also a variety of other bridge groups in Sun City Center and you can see people sitting on their lanais, living rooms or family rooms almost any afternoon or evening of the week PLAYING BRIDGE. The SCC Duplicate Bridge Club has members of all ages, ranging from the middle 50's to the high 90's. The Club sponsors bridge lessons at all levels twice a year. Many beginning students attending these classes fell in love with the game as I did. They later joined our Club and now can be seen playing Duplicate Bridge several times a week. A short time ago I observed four men playing in our Club with an average age of 94 and proud of it.

Only in Sun City Center would you observe such a sight. We have 75 Life Masters in our Club, along with several Bronze, Silver, and Gold Life Masters. The color denotes a plateau of Master Points. Recently, Irene Riha, a lady in her nineties earned enough points to qualify for Life Master status. We are very proud of her.

What is really exciting is to have our grandchildren visit us and while here play Duplicate Bridge. While Duplicate Bridge may have skipped a generation, our grandchildren are learning from us and loving the game.

The SCC Duplicate Bridge association sponsors a sectional bridge tournament under the direction of ACBL Directors each year, the last weekend of February. The Club has done this for the last eight years. People from all over the state come to play and earn Silver points. Silver points can be earned only at Sectional Tournaments, and 25 Silvers are required along with points of various other colors to become a Life Master.

It is a proven fact that bridge tends to keep the mind alert. It is also a satisfying feeling to do well, not for anyone else but for yourself. New players are welcome. We supply a partner if needed.

Hope to see ya'll at the tables. Happy bridging!

The Computer Club, Inc.

by Jack Fischer

The Club began in 1983 when Len Point had a problem with his computer and could not find ready answers. He gathered together the few local "experts" at that time, as sort of a mutual aid society. Club members took turns offering their homes as sites for the monthly meetings.

As the PC became more popular, the Club grew, and moved to ever-larger quarters over the years. In 1988 it became affiliated with the Sun City Center Community Association. Later it incorporated and was granted a 501(c)(3) classification by the IRS, as a tax-exempt educational organization.

Today the Club holds a monthly program meeting in Community Hall at 7:30 PM on the first Wednesday of each month. In addition, Special Interest Groups, which, as the term indicates, specialize in unique aspects of personal computing, meet during the month in separate meetings to concentrate on their interests. These groups include those specializing in genealogy, Windows, Macintosh, Quicken, a beginners group, the Internet and digital imaging.

In 1993, as the result of solid planning and a fortuitous grant, a permanent Computer Learning Center was established in the Kings Point Clubhouse. Subsequently, a second classroom was located in Community Hall. Annually, the Club trains over 1,000 local residents in various aspects of personal computing.

Today, Club membership stands at about 2,000, from both Sun City Center and Kings Point. In addition to being one of the largest clubs in Sun City Center, it is believed to be the largest PC user group in Florida. As the PC continues to gain an ever-growing cadre of users, it is expected that The Computer Club will continue to expand as it fulfills its mission of "Education, Information and Service to the Computer Community of Sun City Center."

Ballroom Dancing at Sun City Center and Kings point

by Dorothy Kolena

When my husband Bob and I moved to Sun City Center 15 years ago we were approached by some of our neighbors with the question, "Are you dancers?" Of course, having danced back in Chicago, we naturally said, "Yes, we dance." Well, that was the start of it. Our good friends Anne and George Rozum were student dance instructors under Carl and Mary Forsberg's tutelage. We asked the Rozums about lessons and they recommended we start in a basic class. Why would we start in the basic class when we already knew how to dance? Why, we had danced all our adult lives. The very idea! Nevertheless, they finally convinced us that would be the way to go. So, albeit reluctantly, we enrolled in the basic class. Well! After a few lessons we discovered we didn't know zilch about dancing properly. Swallowing our pride we found we hadn't been such expert dancers after all.

Two dance clubs were already in existence in Sun City Center when we moved here—the Ballroom Dance Club and the Moonglow club. We joined the Ballroom Dance Club immediately, but had to wait to join Moonglow. They had already reached their full quota of members, but we were finally able to join a year later. In the meantime, another dance club was in its infancy. The Academy of Ballroom Dance was organized, and decided to offer dance classes with the Forsbergs as professional instructors.

Bob and I became active in the Academy, first as Secretary, then as Co-Vice Presidents, and, later, Co-Presidents. After about a year of lessons the Forsbergs asked if we'd like to help out. So we became Student Instructors, joining the Rozums, Jinx and Frank Rives, Homer and Doris Sharp, Anita and Joe O'Connell, Phil and Jean Krause, and Bill and Rose Shanks who now reside at Freedom Plaza. It was quite an experience and very rewarding. We met lots of new and wonderful people, and had loads of fun and laughs to boot.

The experience provided us with many amusing incidents. One I'll always remember involved a couple who came to the dances regularly. Of the two, she would always walk in with the aid of a cane. Once the music started the cane would be propped up against the wall, and off they'd go, dancing the evening away. When the last song played and it was time to leave, she would get her cane and they'd both walk slowly out to their car.

A continuing complaint by prospective students was, "I can't dance because I've got two left feet." Nevertheless, after a few lessons they discovered that wasn't the case after all. Maybe they didn't turn out to be professionals, but they were able to get out on the dance floor and enjoy every minute of it.

Unfortunately my husband, Bob, was only able to enjoy this for five years. Dancing had always been, and still is, my whole life, and losing my dancing partner was devastating. Since replacements were needed, Donna and Art Larson joined the corps of student instructors, replacing Bob and me. Then the Forsbergs asked if I would still continue as part of their team of instructors. Of course I jumped at the chance. It filled a void in my life, gave me something to look forward to, and hopefully helped them bring the joy of ballroom dancing to others. I'm still helping out where and when I can.

Ballroom dancing has continued to be an ever more popular and important activity in Sun City Center and Kings Point. The Singles Club in Sun City Center and Kings Point, the Oldies but Goodies Club have active schedules. Roberta Somerville and Dave Irvin hold classes offering basic instructions with Irvin offering two sessions a week for more advanced dancers. Lefty and Lil Upperman have held practice sessions at Kings Point for years. The SCC Big Band has Tea Dances as well as providing music for other dances and occasions.

So, you can see how ballroom dancing plays a major part in the activities available here in Sun City Center and Kings Point.

The slogan of the Academy of Ballroom Dancing invites you to join and. . .DANCE FOR THE HEALTH OF IT.

Sun City Center Entertainment

by Nick Milano

My wife Mick and I are twelve-year residents of Sun City Center who have enjoyed being deeply involved in entertainment activities in our community. It was natural for us to get involved in this SCC activity since Mick had a background of 35 years in community theatre in the Chicago area. Nick worked behind the scenes.

Each year a new group of retirees join the SCC mainstream. They bring with them experience, talent, and a desire to participate in the many activities. The two of us found our "niche" here in Pelican Players and The Entertainers, and found many new friends and acquaintances as a result.

It took Mick only a few weeks after arrival to audition with The Pelican Players and get a part in "Everybody Loves Opal." She was off and running in a career that has included 9 leads in plays, and appearances in the Follies. I ended up with bit parts, and behind-the-scenes work, and had the privilege of serving as president of the Pelican Players.

Pelican Players was formed some years ago by Shirley Jones. They present two plays and a variety show each year--The Follies--which is the crown jewel of the Pelicans' excellent efforts. The sizable proceeds from the shows are used for scholarships for East Bay and Riverview high school students who go on to study theatre or the fine arts. Rose Ostrander is current president of the Players.

Several years ago it became apparent that a smaller group was needed to entertain around Sun City Center, so the Geublins, Paul Murphy, Enid Clouse, Mick and I, and others of the Pelican Players decided to form The Entertainers. For 12 years this group has performed around SCC for church groups, clubs and nursing homes. Proceeds from their appearances have gone to the Mary Martha House, of Ruskin, a shelter for abused women and children.

A close bond formed between The Entertainers, Sister Margaret of the Mary Martha House, and the children we occasionally entertained. Kids even jumped on stage and performed, much to our delight and the enjoyment of the parents.

Special remembrances: tears we saw in the eyes of the audience at Freedom Plaza when our regular spring presentation was a World War I songfest, with people in the audience singing along with every word; kids hanging onto us at the Mary Martha House, not wanting us to leave; skits about SCC people that hit home to many in the audience; dancing with a little old lady from the audience at one of the performances—who looked up at me and said she was only 90, and was the girl friend of Paul Finnigan who was almost 100. Paul entertained on stage in the Follies until the year he passed on.

Carol Midkiff is current president of The Entertainers. She will welcome volunteers who can make themselves happy by making others happy by participating in the world of entertainment here in Sun City Center.

Sun City Center Emergency Squad

by Jack Frobose

Ray Watson chartered the Emergency Squad in April 1966 with 35 members. They had 53 runs their first year and their only ambulance was a used funeral hearse donated by the Lewers Funeral Home. We understand the population was approximately 4000 in Sun City Center at that time.

As the city grew, so did the number of Squad members, the equipment and the calls to help our residents. Presently our membership has grown to over 300 volunteers, we have four basic life support ambulances, three wheel chair vans, and one deputy captain's car.
The number of calls has increased to record levels. The first six months of 2002 our squad has averaged 1050 calls per month. At that rate we will be near 13,000 for the year. Last year we responded to 11,800 calls.

The average age of our members is 72 years. We also have a group over 80. Every member is dedicated to our motto, "Neighbors helping neighbors," and not one member receives any money for his dedication.

We do not charge for any of our services, and, according to the statistics for last year, as related to what public medical services charge, we saved our community over $2,000,000 in medical costs. Our service is rendered to any of our residents, and any guest in their home. We will take anyone for any type of medical service if they are not able to find normal transportation. The squad is on duty 24 hours each day, 365 days each year. The Squad maintains an inventory of wheel chairs, walkers, crutches and canes that are loaned to our neighbors free of charge. All of our equipment, medical and operational supplies are purchased through the generosity of our residents. No money is supplied from Federal, State or County funds.

A Typical 24 Hour Day

Team Squad members report for duty before 0730 hours. When the Duty Captain acknowledges he has the proper crew, the crew on duty is relieved. The new Duty Captain then issues inspection reports and the crews (ambulance, EMT, with first responder and driver; and van with first responder and driver) proceed to insure that all required equipment is on board, and all warning signals are operative. The vehicles are inspected for cleanliness and damage.

When all vehicles are checked, and the reports are filled out properly, the Duty Captain calls the group together in order to review reports from the Chief, and to review any changes in policies and other information from staff officers. Individual presentations are made for any special awards to team members.

Crews will then sit back to have coffee, relax with the local paper, or personal literature. At mid-morning the Senior EMT, with approval by the Captain, will discuss the training for the day and begin a discussion session. This session will continue with the members available who are not out on call.

During the noon hour lunch is prepared and enjoyed by those available, and kept prepared for those on runs. Mid-afternoon a piece of equipment from one of the vehicles is used for practice and familiarization.

Some teams are scheduled to leave the headquarters building at 1700 hours, except for crews which might still be on runs. In this case the Duty Captain will send the balance of the team home, but will stay in the building until the outstanding crew returns. Other teams stay at the headquarters until later in the evening.

The Captain will insure that all crews scheduled to respond after 1700 will have radios, and have them checked with the night dispatcher before they leave. Once crews have left the building for the day they operate by radio communications from their homes, through the Night Dispatcher. They are relieved the next day at 0730 hours.

Security Patrol—The Eyes and Ears of Sun City Center

by Louis T. Tovey

The SCC Security Patrol is a very sophisticated neighborhood watch system that offers a broad "security blanket" for the entire community. It is a unique organization that many neighborhoods have tried to copy, but so far no place in this county has been able to duplicate it. This is probably due to the amazing spirit of volunteerism that exists in Sun City Center.

The Patrol began as a response by a few residents to a rash of burglaries in the area in 1981. A few SCC men got together and decided to form a neighborhood watch group to protect each others' homes. They used their own cars to patrol the area. It was apparently quite successful in preventing crimes, and grew and grew. Look at them now! More than 1500 volunteers patrol the area an average of ten times a day, day and night—every day of the year! They own five radio-equipped cars. They don't patrol Kings Point because K.P. has a paid Security Department, but they do transport people from Kings Point when no other transportation is available. They also patrol the business and shopping centers within the area.

A volunteer dispatcher in the central office, near the Community Association offices on North Pebble Beach Boulevard, monitors car radios, and answers phone calls from residents, neighbors, the Sheriff's Department, and many others. A review of the types of calls to the Security Office would amaze most residents. Calls are about everything from alligators and lost pets to missing or lost residents. When out-of-state children can't reach their parents by phone, they immediately call the Patrol for help. Stranded motorists frequently call for help, or a ride. Neighbors call about broken sprinklers. Visitors stop in for directions and information. Patrol people have "saved" many people who have locked themselves out of house or car. Drivers supply assistance in cases of flooding, or other emergencies.

The Security Patrol is proud to report that SCC has the lowest crime rate in the County. Sheriff Henderson believes the visibility of Security Patrol cars is largely responsible for deterring crime in the area. The Sheriff's Deputy has informed us that the SCC Patrol responds to several hundred calls every month that they would have had to answer if Patrol members were not available. Residents appreciate the fact that there are trained neighbors available to help them in an emergency.

All dispatchers have the most current information available at their fingertips. They follow a standard operating procedure, so all calls are answered efficiently. Since Patrol cars are always on the road, drivers are able to spot potential trouble spots, and quickly follow dispatcher's requests to help solve problems. One phone call—lots of help.

Some calls are really unusual, and maybe even funny. Unfortunately, all calls do not result in a happy ending. It is pleasant when drivers and dispatchers can say they have had a quiet, boring shift, because that means all is well on the home front, and it's just another calm, beautiful day in Sun City Center.

Here are some unusual calls:

(1) Caller: "There is an alligator knocking at my door! Help!" Patrol car goes to residence, and sure enough, a 7-foot 'gator was banging his tail on the door! As soon as our car put the spotlight on him, the 'gator quickly moved next door. The driver notified the Dispatcher who immediately called the "bounty hunter." The driver kept following the 'gator around the block, but he soon tired of this "game of tag" and slid back into the lake before the hunter arrived.

(2) Caller: Time, 3:45 a.m. "Would you please go to my house and see if I turned the water off in my swimming pool. I am on a trip and I just woke up and realized I forgot to turn the hose off before I left home." Captain answered the call and drove to the house. A block away it was evident that water was running down the street. The pool deck was covered, and the ground next to the house was swamped. Fortunately, water had not got into the home. After turning off the hose and checking the area, the Captain called the owner back to report that all was taken care of. Water had been running 14 hours, so, needless to say, it was a good thing he had called for help.

(3) Caller: "Help! There is a man driving a golf cart on I-75!" Patrol Captain responded. One of SCC's residents had become confused, and actually drove his golf cart onto the Interstate! The resident who had called on his cell phone followed the cart until they were able to get him to pull over. When the Captain arrived on the scene the wanderer had managed to drive 6 miles on the highway. The Captain was able to take the golf cart driver's keys, and report in so the dispatcher could call home and report the wanderer "lost but safe." The dispatcher called the golf cart company to request a pick-up of the cart. The Captain drove the man home in the patrol car, and requested a second patrol car to stand by the cart until it was picked up. A lot of team work was involved, but the story had a happy ending.

* * *

Note from Lou Tovey: "I am really honored to have had an opportunity to serve as Chief of the Patrol for the past year and a half. It has given me the opportunity to work with the most wonderful people in SCC. As far as credit for the success we have, I must share that with the 8 members of the Board of Directors, five Deputy Chiefs, two extremely helpful assistants, 31 Captains, 90 Deputy Captains, and 1545 fantastic volunteers. It is a terrific organization. We would love to have you join us."

VOLUNTEERING IN DEPTH

The Good Samaritans and Samaritan Services

Walter Smith

Back in the early 1980s an association of people joined together to discuss Sun City Center's future, and to discuss possible areas that might need attention. The group was called "Community Coordinating Council." Members of this group were the developer, Kings Point, business, legal, Community Association and Homeowners' Association. It was brought to this group's attention that we had several cases of families who needed financial help for temporary financial problems. Charles D. "Bud" Miller who, at the time, was President of the Civic Association, agreed to investigate and see what was needed.

Along with Lou Ellen Wilson, a Vice President for the developer, and local attorney Frank Riggs, confirmed that help was needed. Shortly, the Good Samaritan Fund was incorporated as a 501-C-3 entity to provide, where needed, financial aid to residents of Greater Sun City Center. A small office in the plaza was opened with Ben Searle as Executive Director, and the Good Samaritans were in business. During its first year, six families who were experiencing financial difficulties received assistance. The help included the payment of utility and pharmacy bills and the purchase (at cost) of special medical-related equipment if recommended by attending physicians. It was a case of neighbors helping each other for the betterment of the community.

Soon it became apparent that other needs existed here such as companion care, or transportation services for those who can't drive. With Doris Healy Ragland as the volunteer Executive Director, a new group called "Samaritan Services" began operation in 1988. Doris, a long-time resident and former nurse, began recruiting additional volunteers and, as a result, many other services were provided to meet the needs of this fast-growing community. In order to accommodate those in wheelchairs who needed to reach hospitals and doctors' offices outside of Greater Sun City Center, a specially-equipped wheelchair van was purchased. As the community grew, more of our older residents needed help getting to hospitals and doctors both locally and in neighboring communities. By 2002, Samaritan Services was operating a wheelchair van and four sedans to transport residents to appointments within a 50 mile radius.

While transportation to hospitals, doctors and medical offices are the large part of our work, we are available for other neighborly assistance such as companion sitting. There are many caregivers in Sun City Center and they need a break from time to time. We have a number of neighbors who provide several hours during the day to caregivers who need relief.

We saw the need to establish an adult day care center and discovered that the former Priest House at the Episcopal Church in Ruskin was available. They agreed to rent it to us for $1.00 a year. Our state representative convinced the state and county to become involved, and now, the state provides the skilled help necessary to operate the center for 30 residents of our area each day.

In the early 90s, an idea for a Drop In Center was suggested. Space in the plaza behind Marie's Beauty Shop became available. Residents seeking companionship and friendly conversation meet there daily now, except Sunday, for coffee and cookies, and to interface with neighbors.

Samaritan Services is also involved with the "Meals on Wheels" program. Residents call us with the type of meals they want, the hospital prepares the food and churches and other organizations around town deliver them to those who request it.

At the turn of the Millennium, the former head of the Sun City Center Security Patrol became involved with Samaritan Services, and set up a new program for residents who needed transportation to stores, shopping, social, medical and other functions within Greater Sun City Center between 9 AM and 4 PM. There are now two vehicles used for this service. Residents who call in are picked up at their home without an advanced reservation and dropped off at their destination. When they are ready to go back home, they just call in again.

We are aware of an increasing need for assistance for residents with Alzheimer's, and their spouses. A support group under the direction of Doris Ragland and Lillian Beaty has been formed and, with great assistance from Dolores Berens, now holds monthly meetings with seminars, speeches and other presentations given by experts.

We have been most fortunate in the gifts we have received from all areas of Greater Sun City Center, the churches, individual wills and many of the clubs in Kings Point and Sun City Center. The business community too has been very generous. This year, for the first time, we conducted a community drive for funds to help support our expanded services.

There are always more things to do than we can accomplish, so there is a continuing need for new people in Samaritan Services. Our office is at 916 North Pebble Beach Blvd and we always welcome people who stop in or to call us at 634-9283.

Lifeline—A Life Saver

by Lewis Riley

Dorothy Osborne lives alone in Sun City Center. She is in her eighties. She is a participant in Lifeline. Her next door neighbor is Marcia Dake, a retired dean of two nursing colleges, who is part of the Lifeline chain that helps protect people like Ms. Osborne. Here's how Marcia Dake reported one of Lifeline's life-saving incidents:

"At approximately six o'clock, one morning, I received a call from Lifeline to see if I would check on Mrs. Osborne since she had not "checked in" at her usual early hour. I went to her home and found her on the floor in her screened room behind the carport. Mrs. Osborne had taken the garbage can to the street, and as she set it down, she fell, and was unable to get up. She crawled clear up the driveway, through the carport, into the screened room, and passed out. Without Lifeline, and their call to me, it is an open guess as to how long she would have lain on the floor. The Emergency Squad was called by Lifeline as I tried to make her more comfortable. Her right hip had fractured, and she later required surgery."

Dora Richardson, who also lives alone in Sun City Center, wrote to the Men's Club—sponsor of Lifeline—expressing her appreciation for the protection Lifeline recently afforded her. Here is her story:

"Lifeline came to my assistance twice when I became ill during the night—thus saving my life. The persons who answered my calls were very caring and helpful until I was taken to the hospital." Ms. Richardson has a condition called Myasthenia Gravis which causes muscle weakness. She blacks out with no prior warning, and when she wakens she needs assistance to become mobile again. Twice, when this happened, she used her Lifeline signal device, and feels it was critical to her survival. She feels very secure in knowing there are neighbors who can be called to come to her aid, along with the Emergency Squad, through the Lifeline communications system.

Lifeline is administered by the Men's Club of SCC. The Club makes available to Lifeline subscribers small portable wireless devices, which will send a distress signal, or just a check-in--"All is well"--signal, through the telephone system, to the Lifeline control center in Boston. The Boston headquarters knows their clients are expected to check in daily with the OK signal, Lifeline has a record of neighbors, or others nearby, who can be called on to visit the client to see if anything is wrong. "Clients" can also send an emergency signal on the Lifeline device, and the Boston headquarters can arrange for local help from neighbors or other rescue facilities. There is a modest monthly charge for the service. The Lifeline program was initiated in 1990, and the service provider, Lifeline Systems, Inc., of Boston, was recommended by Herb Lewis, a retired hospital administrator. The number of subscribers increased from 48 at the end of 1993 to over 270 in the year 2002, and the Men's Club volunteer staff stands, now, at over 30. Lewis Riley is the V.P. of the SCC Men's Club who oversees the Lifeline program, and he is assisted by 34 Men's Club Voluntary Installation Persons (V.I.P.s) and a part time office manager, Mrs. Shirley Spittle.

The Community Foundation of Greater Sun City Center *

by Sally B. Hahn

The Community Foundation of Greater Sun City Center is a division of the Community Foundation of Tampa Bay. The local council awards grants with the goals of improving the lives of area residents and adhering to the wishes of our donors. Funds within the Foundation may be established by individuals, families, corporations, or non-profit agencies.

A major goal of the Foundation this year has been enhancing the education of our area school children. Cypress Creek, Ruskin and Wimauma elementary schools have received funds to purchase computers, software, and books to promote reading readiness and progress. Cypress Creek was able to buy Spanish-English dictionaries for fourth grade students. A pilot forensics program was launched at East Bay High School and instruments were added to the music department of Eisenhower Middle School.

Although the Community Foundation and the Community Association are totally unrelated, the Foundation has recently made numerous grants to clubs which are moving to new or larger quarters and need to add equipment or storage. Several donors have stipulated that their funds be used for projects within Sun City Center.

The Board of Directors of the Foundation

*** A grant was received from the Foundation in support of this publication.**

Friends of Hospice/Life Path Hospice

by Lee Albrecht

A Hospice House is a place where a person with a life-limiting illness can be cared for in a warm, home-like, peaceful environment when no caregiver is available at home. A group of Sun City Center residents recognized the need for such a facility and first met on March 21, 1994. Destined to be a mostly volunteer effort, they elected Jocelyn Mather as president, Ray Purcell, V.P., Dick May, Treasurer and myself as secretary of the organization to be known as Friends of Hospice--eventually changed to Life Path Hospice. It is a not-for-profit organization, is supported mostly by volunteers, and depends greatly on donations and fund-raising efforts to finance its existence.

Pastor Robert Gingery of SCC's United Community Church was an early supporter of the Hospice effort, around 1985, and the Church donated office space at the start when the patient load was six to eight. Life Path Hospice and Palliative Care had an office in Sun City Plaza and served an average of 80 families.

Now, through the relentless efforts of the Board and other volunteers and local organizations, Life Path Hospice has moved into their own "home," on American Eagle Drive, celebrated by a dedication ceremony on August 9, 2001. The House, designed to provide a home-like environment, has eight bedrooms, each decorated differently, with a most-functional patient bed, and a convertible lounge chair/bed so a family member can stay in the room. There is a family room, residential-type kitchen, and a chapel. Family and friends are encouraged to visit as they would at home. The first patient was admitted on September 5, 2001, and since then over 100 patients have been cared for in the new facility.

Support of local organizations for Hospice has been phenomenal. In the first year there were: Women's Golf Tournaments at the North Course; golf outings at Cypress Greens and Kings Point golf courses; Charity Bridge Parties; a Christmas card sale; and the Hospice Hustle, a walk for Hospice. Through the years, many groups donated funds to Hospice; the Tennis Group through a very successful senior tournament; SCC Swim Team; Kings Point Water Rhythms; Knights of Columbus; Lion's Club; the Art Club; Garden Club; Sam Kupper's "Sunday Afternoons at Kings Point;" many church organizations; and local merchants. Funds were raised through Sun City Center Big Band Concerts, as Ms. Senior City Center pageant winners added a touch of glamour, circulating in the lobby.

Late in 1997 the parcel of land on which the new building stands was donated by The Freedom Group, developers of Freedom Plaza and Plaza West Assisted Living.

"You matter because you are you. You matter to the last moment of your life—and we will do all we can, not only to help you die peacefully, but to live until you die." Dame Cecily Saunders.

Interfaith Cooperation

by Ken Barringer, Ph.D

One of the real achievements of the residents of Sun City Center is their work on interfaith cooperation. It started years ago when several SCC churches, observing the need to provide a variety of services to the people of adjacent communities, decided to combine their efforts. United Community Church had been offering sewing classes for adults, and a tutoring program in the elementary school. Prince of Peace Catholic Church had worked with migrants in Ruskin and with the Happiness Center for Retarded Children in Ruskin. And the St. Andrew Presbyterian Church had demonstrated interest in helping with the tutoring program in Wimauma.

In January, 1971 the three congregations combined their efforts and agreed to an organizational meeting in September of that year when the Christian Social Action Council was born. They have met from that time on a continuing basis, and were later joined by the Jewish congregation at which time the name was changed to Interfaith Council of Sun City Center. Its aim was "to promote the health, welfare and the education of deserving persons in Sun City Center and its environs." Clergy of each congregation are "members at large," but don't have voting power.

The first of the money-making efforts to support the Council's goals was a rummage sale in October, 1971 in the Wimauma Civic Building. They then started the popular and very successful Nearly New Shop in Wimauma in 1974, and have recently moved it into space in SCC's Shopping Plaza. There were also drives to collect used paper, aluminum cans and cardboard which until recently resulted in modest income.

A key project of the Council that has grown over the years is its high school scholarship program to award scholarships to deserving seniors of East Bay High School.

The tutoring program for elementary students in schools located near Sun City Center has continued to grow and evolve. Volunteers work closely with teachers and the school administrator to match students' needs with the abilities of those who volunteer their time. Other volunteers work with students, but Council volunteers have the longest record of consistent service to anxious children. Our volunteers tell us that they, themselves are the benefactors as they become excited when they see how their simple tasks help and motivate the students they serve.

Meals on Wheels and the Hot Lunch Program for Seniors in Wimauma were first launched by the Interfaith Council. They also helped to spearhead the County Medical Center in Ruskin, the development of South Bay Hospital, and the Garden Project, which consisted of the planting of trees to beautify the community.

Council members have consistently supported the Mary Martha House in Ruskin, the Good Samaritans, the Hospice program, the Emergency Squad, the Redlands Migrant Ministry, and the Beth El Mission. The Council has stirred the excitement of its members by raising money and volunteering their services to Habitat for Humanity to build homes for needy families.

An important source of income for the Interfaith Council has been the Big Band Concert each December. But the largest source of income is the Nearly New Shop whose recent move into the Sun City Center Plaza has made it easier for people to donate clothes, electronics, jewelry, and other things, and is attracting a fast-growing clientele.

A strong feeling of mutual respect and understanding among the eight congregations now joined with the Council has had significant benefits. Over all it has been a fine example of “faith in action.” The Interfaith Council has demonstrated that “people of the book” can take their faith seriously, and can “love their neighbors as themselves.”

Currently, the congregations that make up The Interfaith Council are Prince of Peace Catholic Church, St. Andrew Presbyterian Church, St. John the Divine Episcopal Church, Trinity Baptist Church, United Methodist Church, United Community Church, The Jewish Congregation, and Redeemer Lutheran Church.

The above represent the bulk of faith communities of Sun City Center, and the Interfaith Council stands ready to welcome others.

Sun City Gadabouts (Travel Club)

George Flowers

The Sun City Gadabouts celebrated their 20th Anniversary in 2002. The Gadabouts was organized in February 1982 with a membership of 40 people. Today the membership, limited to members of the Sun City Center Community Association, is near 2000. In the early days of the Gadabouts the trips were only day trips, no overnight trips. One of the first trips was to the water reclamation station on El Rancho near Ojai Street (now the site of a church). Can you imagine doing a trip there today?

The Gadabouts has been very fortunate in having only four presidents. The first president and organizer of the Gadabouts was Mary Crest, followed by Frank Zaeick and his wife Marie, who ran the Gadabouts until Frank passed away in 1998. Marie took over the presidency and ran it until 2000 when George Flowers and his wife Roz took over and are currently in charge.

The Gadabouts is a non-profit organization and, therefore, they can obtain the best prices available since there are no overhead expenses. The Gadabouts is a great tribute to the community, offering a service for those who are unable to travel on their own. All the Gadabouts trips are escorted and the prices include transportation from Sun City Center, gratuities, taxes, entrance fees and a good time! Also, all the officers and board members of the Gadabouts are volunteers.

The Gadabouts have traveled from the east coast to the west coast, from the Caribbean to Canada, Alaska, Hawaii, Great Britain, the Baltic and Mediterranean Seas, and many local day trips to dinner theatres, performing arts centers, theme parks and other fun places. The Gadabouts members are lifelong learners who enjoy art museums and historical locations.

At a recent Gadabouts meeting, a trip was introduced for a new dinner theatre. One member asked, "Is dinner included at the dinner theatre?" Assurance was given. Another time, after introducing a *Mystery Trip*, a member asked, "Where are we going on the mystery trip?" It was answered in a whisper, "It's a mystery."

The Gadabouts are well-seasoned travelers who enjoy a good time. Whether traveling on a train, airplane or bus, you can always hear laughter and a lot of conversation. And, of course, there's that occasional sound of someone sleeping.

George and Roz

Coffee and Conversation "Expanding Our Horizons"
by Paul Robbins

"Use it or lose it" was a phrase frequently quoted by Dr. Robert Gingery when he was

Senior Minister of United Community Church. He is a great believer in education—keeping the mind busy.

In 1976 Dr. Gingery encouraged the Christian Education Board of UCC to start the Church College. It has been a great success. But the College only holds classes during week days, and only six weeks in the fall and six weeks in the spring. Even with the College there were too many who were "losing it!" Too many were not using the College, or not using it enough. Dr. Gingery recognized that in a twenty minute sermon on Sunday morning he could not give the spiritual stimulus needed, and also have time for desired intellectual stimulation. Thus, again, he encouraged the Christian Education Board to start the Coffee and Conversation series of educational meetings in the early 1990s.

As with the College, Coffee and Conversation has been successful. This series seeks to enhance our understanding and inform us about topics important to us in our personal lives, in our Christian faith, and in the community. Each Sunday's topic is presented by a knowledgeable speaker, and participation by the audience is encouraged. Members of the community who are not members of the Church are welcome to attend, and some do attend.

A sample of programs that have been presented recently are: What is Life all About?; Aging Successfully; How to Get Along With Your Doctor; The Hungry People of Hillsborough County: Who? Where? Why?; Sun City Center History—Part 1; Tampa Bay, Paradise at Risk; Why are Americans Becoming Interested in Buddhism?; The Story of Wimauma; Listening to Your Inner Voice. Programs are presented in Great Hall of United Community Church on Sunday, from 10:45 to 11:45 AM from mid-October to May 1, holidays excepted. During the period from January 1, 2001 to January, 2002 a total of 28 programs were presented in the Coffee and Conversation series. Average attendance was 73 per meeting. About 25% of the meetings were primarily religious education. Another 25% dealt mainly with health problems. About 21% involved book reviews, and/or general information. Some 11% dealt with broader Church issues. Four per cent involved environmental issues. The mix of topics varies from year to year.

A companion program, "Issues and Ideas," primarily started and run by Phil Lange, who has organized over 600 of these weekly sessions, with meetings held at Lake Towers, is co-sponsored by United Community Church and Lake Towers.

Sun City Center is a great place where many stay active and fit by participation in sports, arts and crafts, and club activities. However, Community Church College, Coffee and Conversation, and Issues and Ideas also indicate that many are also interested in keeping fit mentally.

The Sun City Center Library
A Report from the Librarian, Lee Hohmann

The Sun City Center Library is a private library - a tax-exempt, non-profit organization. The library has become a valuable asset to the community. Number of patrons has increased dramatically in the last five years. Most active patrons are our own community members, the rest coming from Freedom Plaza, Lake Towers, Courtyards, Kings Point, and a few from Ruskin, Wimauma and Apollo Beach.

The spirit of volunteerism is very strong in the library. Technology has brought new duties to traditional library jobs. We have converted our old library card catalogue system to computerized systems, and our circulation into an automated system as well. The Librarian, four part-time staff members, and 41 volunteers, have helped a lot during the conversion to the new technology of computers. Everyone participated in bar-coding all library materials, including Community Association cards.

There are five computers; two for checking materials, one for checking in. There are two available to patrons to allow them to search through the many materials available to them. The circulation desk is manned by the part-time library staff. They work as a team because they know that teamwork needs to be built into library skills.

The Library provides a large collection of both fiction and non-fiction books, with at least 12,000 regular print books, 775 large print books, 2,110 videotapes, 2,224 paperbacks, and 874 audio-casettes. Many library materials were donated by our own residents, as well as "Friends of the Library." Over 14,000 materials are being checked out every month, and at least 450 items are borrowed from the Tampa Hillsborough Library.

It is not only books and audiovisual materials that are significant in the library. It also provides access to a total of 38 titles of magazine subscriptions, and four financial newspaper publications, plus a few collections of books and videotapes for children. Puzzles are also a popular part of the collections as well.

The library offers many excellent services. There are two public-access computers that help patrons access the collections of Tampa's Hillsborough Public Library. Patrons can reserve any materials from these two public access computers and have items delivered to our Library. Talking books for the visually impaired are also available from the Tampa Hillsborough Public Library without charge.

One of the sources of daily income is our own Book Sale Room. It is open every day, and everyone is welcome to purchase anything displayed there. The other major sources of income are voluntary individual donations from members of the community, "Friends of the Library," local service clubs and organizations. Part of the income also comes from the SCC Community Association. This financial support has allowed the Sun City Center Library to acquire more and more library materials, and to become a superb community library.

THE CLOCK
by Bob Wicklund

Life is a journey. We work and work to raise our children and acquire "things" and then without our choosing or warning life takes a dreadful turn. Without accepting it or agreeing that it is even happening, a life is slowly brought to an end. Follow me now to see how this took place:

Lois and Bob

Tick…tock…tick…tock. Why? Tell me why he had to go and buy that clock? It's about 10 ten inches round and it sits over the bedroom door where I can see it from where I am lying in my hospital bed here at home. And it makes that loud tick…tock sound. I don't like that. It was so nice when he was sleeping in the hospital bed next to me, (we each slept on a hospital bed, he didn't want me to feel singled out) so I could simply call over and ask him, "What time is it?" And he would gradually wake up, grope around and tell me the time. Generally it was around two or three in the morning. You see I was spending most of the day in bed sleeping. So I would wake up in the middle of the night and start to wonder, "Am I going to live till morning?" I needed reassurance.

It never used to be this way. Why, when we came to SCC back in 1987 we had a brand new house and a swimming pool to boot! That was so exciting for me. Yes, I laid down the law. If we were going to build a new house in SCC, I was going to have a pool and so we did. Not only that, every thing was on one floor. It was so great, I didn't have to run down to the basement from the third floor to wash and dry clothes. We don't even have to go down to the basement to get to the garage; every thing is on one floor. This is really neat.

And the neighbors were great. We had picnics together, pitch in dinners, went to shows together, they were real friends. They encouraged us to join the dance clubs, take ballroom dance lessons. And I did very well at that. Bob, well, he tried and with my help did pretty good. But there is that incessant clock again. Tick…tock…tick…tock. Something seems to be wrong with me. I seem to be having trouble walking now. I'll have to start to use a three wheeled walker.

We go to the Mayo Clinic. Surely after looking at the MRI they will be smart enough to figure out what is wrong, you know, have the magic bullet. Sadly it wasn't to be. The Monster must be slowly creeping through my brain. And then I fall and shatter my L2 vertebrae. That takes eight weeks to mend and I end up with a nasty blood clot (DVT) in my leg but I still got around with my walker. At least for awhile.

Now that I think back, it was sneaking up. I always thought that I would get better but somehow I went from a power wheel chair to a plain one simply because I now needed total help. What's going on here? I try to do all my exercises but still…..

Tick...tock…tick…tock---damn that clock. Breathing is a problem now. It's pneumonia. They tell me I am my own worst enemy that I don't know how to swallow any more. That's a surprise to me. They say food is slipping by and going down into my lungs and that causes pneumonia. Their answer, no more food by mouth, put in a PEG tube, you know, poke a hole through the abdominal and stomach wall and stick in a tube through which they can pour nutrients. That was a tough change. The one thing that Bob and I were enjoying together, eating, was stolen from us. My cans of liquid nutrients came three times a day but Bob had to hide from me at meal time because if I was present while he was eating I would literally beg for a bit of mashed potatoes or a bit of carrot from his plate. And he would have to say no. He couldn't handle that.

Tick…tock…tick…tock. My lungs are acting up again. I am getting weak. Why is this? What have I done, I want to live. Hold on, Emergency Squad is at the door and we are on our way to the hospital. Well, I won't have to listen to that darn clock now. But it is getting so hard to breathe. My chest hurts they keep poking this tube down my nose and it hurts like hell. "Sorry honey, this will only take a few more minutes", the nurse tells me. But I am ready to scream but I can't because I am so very weak. I am aware that Bob is holding my hand but I am so very, very tired that I know that I must be dying and then…..I just quit breathing and it is the end.

WHY MOVE TO SUN CITY CENTER
by Edmund Hansen

Why move to Sun City Center? I'm sure reasons vary as much as individuals who comprise the whole. And our story? Here it is.

My wife's parents were the first to leave the frozen tundra of Wisconsin, finally settling down in Dunedin, Florida. During spring break we would load the station wagon and head for Grandma and Grandpa. So you see, we were familiar with the greater Tampa area, the beaches and theme parks.

As I entered my late fifties, our family encountered some of life's road bumps which soon escalated to tragedy status. Our third of four sons returned with full blown AIDS. We were the caregivers for his final fifteen months. The stress left both of us in emotional and physical shambles.

My wife, Ginny, wanted to recuperate near her parents who now lived in Lakeland. She flew to Lakeland to procure an apartment. But before she finalized the contract, word was received from the Army with news that our oldest son was seriously wounded in Samalia.

Ginny secured air passage for the next day to return to Wisconsin. While biding time she decided to drive to the Bradenton beaches to spend some quiet time. Passing exit 46 on I-75, she remembered an advertisement about Sun City Center. Pulling off the highway she paid a visit. Later she would tell me, "I knew immediately that is where we would retire."

After our son was out of danger and safely back in the States, Ginny rented a furnished condo in Kings Point for the winter. I arranged my vacation to be able to spend Christmas with her in Sun City Center.

I arrived at Tampa International Airport at 5 P.M. December 17, 1993 with an outside temperature of 75 Fahrenheit. A far cry from the Wisconsin temperature I had just left. Arriving, feeling ill, my condition went from bad to worse. With a crashed immune system and excruciating joint pain, the physician soon recommended my immediate retirement as a physically disabled person. I followed his orders. We moved our possessions as quickly as possible to Sun City Center.

I turned to writing as a hobby which resulted in the publishing of two books, one magazine article and five articles in the Tampa Tribune. In my first book, titled, A Father's Story: the story of a son's battle with AIDS, I wrote about our arrival in Sun City Center.

We chose Sun City Center because it is less than fifty miles from Ginny's parents in Lakeland and her only sibling in Clearwater. Since it is a retirement community many have experienced the Lord's comfort. They have opened their arms to us with our hurts. At this point in our lives, we need that for emotional healing.And these great people did take us in and comforted us.

My Dreams Have Come True!
by Judie Krody

As I was nearing retirement I made a list of things I wanted to do upon moving to Sun City Center: volunteer work, exercise, further education, and fun. I was a technical manager at AT&T, and also published a newsletter, monthly, for several departments where I worked. My biggest wish was that I could find a volunteer spot on a local paper in Sun City Center. A year after we moved into our new home I was asked to join the News of Sun City Center, and am now Co-editor of that fine publication, working with a terrific group of people. My dreams have come true!

Married to the Place
by Ray and Ruth Anderson

Ray and I came to Sun City Center in late December, 1988, as newlyweds, and moved into our duplex in the Fairview section on New Year's Eve. We both had sold our homes—Ray in Illinois, and Ruth in North Carolina—so we spent several weeks shopping for furniture, and getting settled. We quickly became involved with activities, including Security Patrol, dance clubs, bowling, Men's Club, Lifeline, Hospice volunteering. We have made many friends here, and think SCC is a pretty special place. We're happy we chose it for our retirement years.

A TRANSITIONAL FOCUS

by **Bob Wicklund**

Men have always had an affection for the sea, especially when it comes to sailing. You use your knowledge and skills to harness the power of the wind. It's a good feeling when you have mastered the skill. But now, why in heck is some guy from Sun City Center talking about the sea? What's going on here?

For me it was kind of like a dream come true. We had searched the Tampa and Pinellas county areas during vacations for five years looking for a potential retirement community. Finally we discovered Sun City Center and it was very nice. But when I discovered the Tampa Sailing Squadron (TSS) in Apollo Beach where you had access to the Tampa Bay and the Gulf of Mexico and it was just 25 minutes from SCC, that was it. Lois (wife) loved SCC and was not exactly a gung ho sailor but if her nutty husband found pleasure in sailing, well, it was his retirement too.

TSS wasn't a yacht club but rather a bunch of men who bent their energies to various tasks around a sailing club as a way of repairing and building as the need arose to keep costs down. It was a way to make owning a boat and the sport of sailing affordable for the average interested boater. Notice the use of the term "sailing club". Power boats (stink potters) were not allowed. This was just the kind of sail club we were interested in (and could afford).

We did our share of cruising, not long cruises down to the Keys or out to the Bahamas like some members. No, ours were generally short over night affairs. But it was fun. You shared your voyage with others (just like the folks in sun City Center, were concerned, ready to step up and help if you experienced a problem). But the cruising, even the day sailing came to an end when my First Mate developed balance problems. The balance problem increased in severity until in three years she slipped off into eternity.

So my poor boat (named Patience, by the way) sat at the dock for almost three years. To keep the barnacles from building up I arranged for a diver to bi-monthly scrape and clean the bottom. That helped. But now, without my First Mate, single handling my 33 foot Morgan with her high freeboard, where the wind can easily throw you off course as you try to head into your slip, well, I just didn't feel comfortable with that. Even with extra hands on board bringing her into the slip can sometimes be a Chinese fire drill. Floundering in the slip where there is the potential to damage your neighbor's boat is not too sharp. Anyway, in the past six months my energies have turned to helping TSS with race committee duties where Patience can be used effectively. So what's so great about race committee duties? Let me shed some light on that subject.

Sail boat owners and their crews who race competitively can be an aggressive nutty bunch. And when I say that I tend to compare them to myself who would normally head for the dock quickly when black clouds appear on the horizon. But that's not the style of sailboat racers. In the past, at times when foul weather sprang up suddenly, the fleet has experienced knock downs, broken masts and blown out sails, but no injuries. The competitive spirit thrives among them. However, the stout heartedness of the racing fleet does tend to impinge on the race committee boat staff. Let me describe it.

It was the first part of August, bright and sunny when we left the dock in an 18 foot run about that we use to set up the race course. Just the two of us would conduct the race that day. By the way, conducting the race requires a very carefully scheduled time sequence that involves raising and lowering signal flags at very specific time increments in conjunction with horn sounds. The actual race start time is specified in the race instructions. We set a starting line using a two foot diameter orange ball (with anchor) for one end of the line. It is located at a point whose distance is based on a calculation involving the number of boats racing and average boat length. An orange flag positioned on our port gunnel defines our end of the line. Our boat is anchored and the line is set perpendicular to the wind to give the racers a windward start. Let it be known that the individual captains are very, very aware of our signals and try to position themselves to cross the start line the instant the final flag is lowered and the horn sounds. It is important to be at the theoretical starting line the instant the race starts but…if a boat is over early, it must turn around, go back over the start line, come about and start over. That is a heavy time penalty because in many races boats often finish seconds apart. So in addition to keeping track of the exact time sequence and handling the signal flags we must keep a sharp eye on the start line in order to identify an over early boat. But again I digress.

That day in August the eight boats completed the first race and we got the second race started in fine fashion, no potential protests against the race committee. However, there was one thing that concerned me. Dark clouds had been forming over the land mass. I said to my partner, (while there was some vague rumbling way off in the distance) "Eric," I said, "that storm looks like it might get to us." "Don't worry, Bob," Eric said confidently, "I've been around Tampa Bay a long time and that storm's going to stay over the land mass." Time passes. Guess what, it is now starting to rain and it is starting to get very dark. The fleet is beginning to finish the second race. The rain is really starting to drive hard now. Boats are crossing the finish line with jibs furled and main sheets reefed. We can barely see the last boat as it crosses the finish line. And now the wind is **screaming** at us. The driving rain has turned the water into a boiling mass of gray foam. Lightning crackles around us. Three times Eric went forward to try and pull the anchor but was driven back from the bow by the thunderous cracks of lightning and thunder. Eric is strong, powerfully built, but he is no match for that lightning. Finally there is a brief lull and he manages to get the anchor up. Meanwhile, I am in the stern, bailing out the continuing deluge of rain water which has caused the stern to sink such that sea water is ready to pour into the boat over the transom. Finally Eric gets the out board started and the forward motion of the boat will cause the water to drain out through the scuppers after I remove the two plugs at the bottom of the transom.

Meanwhile, I am suffering a personal calamity, I am shaking and shivering from the exposure of the cold driving rain. Stupid me, I failed to bring foul weather gear. Fortunately, Eric is unaffected by all this rain, he weighs 290 pounds so he has built in protection. Me, I feel like I must be close to hypothermia, literally shaking like a leaf. I couldn't wait to get to the club house where the guys wrapped me in towels and provided hot coffee.

And so the day ended successfully with two races in, recorded, and everybody back safely. It was a great day at TSS.

Thanksgiving, Not the Old Fashioned Way

by Edith R. Pray

In the summer of 1987 my husband and I made the transition from northern living to southern living. We moved into our new home in Sun City Center and began to explore the Gulf Coast of Florida. We discovered Sarasota and its beautiful beaches as we commenced our volunteer work at the Mote Marine Science Center and Aquarium. This love affair with Sarasota has continued for fifteen years.

That first Thanksgiving in Florida my husband and I departed from tradition and decided to take our Thanksgiving dinner to the beach. The now familiar route along Interstate 75 took us over the Manatee Rivers, through fragrant orange groves, and past two discount shopping malls. It led us past the airport and the Ringling Museum complex, to the Intracoastal Waterway. As was usually the case, we were to discover, the drawbridge was raised, and long lines of cars stood at attention as small boats with tall masts sailed through.

As we waited, I wondered if the manatees had begun their seasonal trek in from the chilly waters of the Gulf to the warmer upstream rivers and power plants. I wished them well on this difficult trip as they encountered man-made dangers along the way in the form of speed-boats and careless navigators. Around us, pelicans, alert for the catch of the day, hovered over the fishermen who dotted the piers on each side of the bridge. The bridge slowly descended, clinked shut, and the flow of traffic passed onto Bird Key and St. Armands Circle.

Designed by John Ringling in 1925 to be a world-class shopping district, the Circle was lovely with its lush tropical foliage. Tucked among the bougainvillea, oleander and hibiscus, Italian Baroque statuary was showcased. The pricey stores and restaurants which surrounded the Circle twinkled with little lights, and the traditional Christmas decorations. It was the only point of reference to the time of year. Certainly the eighty-five-degree temperature gave no indication that we had only thirty-one more shopping days until Christmas.

Continuing around the Circle, we headed for Lido Beach. The parking was no problem, and the beach was easily accessed by boardwalks which crossed the dunes. Sea oats and palm trees fringed the beach. The sand was clean and white, and stretching before us was eight hundred miles of aquamarine water that reached to the Mexican coastline. Laughing gulls daintily tip-toed across the sand, their soft gray and white feathers ruffled by the breeze. Five pelicans flew overhead in formation. Children built sand castles at the water's edge, and sun worshipers, bronze and glistening, gave themselves to the noon day sun.

I thought back to other Thanksgivings in the wintry Midwest, where I rose at dawn to stuff an eighteen pound turkey, prepared vegetables, mashed potatoes, made gravy, rolled pie crust, polished silver, and set a festive table. While I struggled in the kitchen, my husband shoveled snow, lugged up wood for the fireplace, carried out trash, popped corn, and drove to the airport on icy roads. We were young and full of energy, and eager to build a sense of permanence and tradition for our children.

But, now we are not so young, and our children are intent on building their own family traditions. We choose to live in Sun City Center, Florida, thousands of miles from their homes. Traveling north at this time of year does not top our list of favorite things to do.

I unpack our Thanksgiving dinner from the cooler. It consists of turkey sandwiches, made from white meat and thin, whole wheat bread; salt-free potato chips; cranberry relish; a plastic bottle of cider; and pumpkin pie made with egg whites and low-fat evaporated milk. "Hurrah for the pumpkin pie!"

It all tastes delicious, and we feel positively carefree as we sip our cider, eat our healthful dinner, toss a few crumbs to a friendly herring gull, then throw our paper plates into the trash can.

So, over the river and through the palm trees and orange groves of Florida, to the beach we go. Is this the beginning of a new tradition? I certainly hope so.

I FOUND THE FOUNTAIN OF YOUTH

by Ty Sturdevant

In 1994 we arrived in Sun City Center and immediately knew that this was the place we wanted to be for our retirement. At that time I was moderately overweight, but looked forward to playing occasional golf and tennis. Like most persons I began outrageously, spraying my golf balls and hitting the tennis ball erratically.

By 1998, however, things were starting to come into focus. I don't know what caused it but I started having unlimited energy. Perhaps it was the drink I had at the Fountain of Youth at St. Augustine. Or maybe it was the vitamin supplements we were starting to take or our healthier diet. We no longer ate snacks and had fruit for dessert instead of ice cream. Or, do you think it could be the inspiration I received from my fellow golfers and tennis players? Or was it just the friendly waves from people passing by?

In any event, I started to feel energetic and my golf and tennis games started improving. I entered the Hillsborough Senior Games and won gold medals in the 50 and 100 yard dashes (against many totally unfit seniors.) I met a real track star, Murrell Loy, 13 years my senior, who urged me to compete in real senior games. I convinced my wife that in-line skating wasn't the most dangerous hobby I could have, though she drew the line at bungy jumping.

The result? I was twenty pounds lighter and started to run at every chance I found. My golf handicap dropped, and my tennis game improved. But the most dramatic result was that I was competing in track meets in the dash events. I had never run track in high school or college and I had no training advice or practice. I just ran on the golf course while playing as much as I could and dashed after errant tennis ball on the court. Once a week I would rollerblade for an hour, about ten miles.

And how about the results? At the track meets? Even against men who had run over the years I could compete. Sometimes gold medals, often silver, but almost always some medal. And, instead of competing in only the 100 and 200 meter dashes, I added the 400 meters and, finally this year, the 800 meters.

Mysteriously, even though I normally play golf six days a week, tennis three days, and my roller blading plus swimming every day, I just don't get aches or pains! Is this because of the joint medication I take or is it because I dash to the mail box, into the grocery store, on the golf course, or on the tennis court? Who knows?

Right now, as a 74 year old, I feel like I am in a teenage body. It may not last long and I admit that we are all mortals, but every day I am thankful that somehow, at least temporarily, I have found The Fountain of Youth.

IT'S A NEIGHBORLY THING

By Tricia Smith

In 1982 as Sun City Center spread rapidly north, Gene and Dawn Merz snapped up the last two duplex lots on Columbine Place – one for them and one for Dawn's sister and brother-in-law, Madeline and Ron Rose.

Everyone on the cul-de-sac was new and in about the same circumstances – newly retired and ready to enjoy the " Golden Years" together in Florida. They played golf and tennis together; they joined churches, volunteered at the hospital, the Emergency Squad, the Security Patrol. They joined dance clubs and clubs to pursue their individual interests but above all they were good neighbors and became fast friends.

Very suddenly it seemed that health problems cropped up and before long there were unexpected deaths to contend with. Naturally everyone rallied round with the customary casseroles and consolation but when the immediacy of their shock passed there was much loneliness to be confronted.

Stan and Dorothy Anderson thought of getting some of the neighbors on the cul de sac together on Monday evenings to go to dinner, mainly to make sure the new widowers, including Gene Merz, were not allowed to be hermits. There were widows also and they too were enfolded in the neighborly embrace on Monday evenings.

Several of the houses of Columbine Place like ours have new owners and we were delighted to be invited to join the group on Mondays. It's been a four year habit now for the original group and one that we look forward to be addicted to. We're really getting acquainted and we're thankful to the Andersons who started the ball rolling as a neighborly thing.

Harry and Tricia

Onward and Upward
by Edward Tucker Smith

Well, it's 5 PM Eastern Daylight Time, in Sun City Center, Florida, August 4, 2002, and I'm sitting here at my computer, contemplating the absurdity of it all—because if I live another seven hours I will have reached the ripe old age of EIGHTY—80, that is—if anyone can believe that.

August 5th, 1922 was the fateful day, and I remember it well. Well—not quite. The earliest memory I have is being held in my mother's arms, looking out the kitchen window in Pine Bluff, Arkansas. If she was holding me, I couldn't have been more than about 2 or 2-1/2, so I can honestly say that I have a recall of at least 76 or 77 years. But I can't remember what I had for lunch today.

Like many others, I'm not in perfect health, of course. I can't make that claim, but I still have all of the hair on my head, which is more than most SCC guys can claim. My waist line can still be encircled by a 36-inch belt, and I can make my way through two sets of tennis doubles without panting too heavily. My eyes are 20-20 with my bifocals on, and the verdict last week, from the optometrist, was that I have no sign of either glaucoma or macular degeneration. My hearing is perfect—with the help of two hearing aids, of course, and my most recent wife hasn't moved out—yet. I don't fly aircraft anymore, but I wouldn't hesitate to barrel into the soup and go on the gauges for an hour or so in at least mild turbulence, and shoot an ILS approach under a 300-foot ceiling.

Other than all of the above, though, I suppose I, like any 80-year-old, must admit that I'm approaching the inevitable, especially considering the presence of Non-Hodgkins lymphoma, but the heart doctor says the ticker is pounding away with the steadiness of Joe Jones on drums. I'm not really too worried about the hot breath of the grim reaper, though, 'cause I reminded Linda, just today, that she promised to stick around 'til the inevitable happened, and she agreed—and our wonderful pets, Gizmo and Aeriel, were my witnesses.

So, in the spirit of a John Phillip Sousa march—ONWARD AND UPWARD!!!!

PART TWO

A PHOTO COLLECTION OF SUN CITY CENTER

Its People, Lifestyle, Clubs,

Activities, Facilities, and

Environments

Life In Sun City Center

A PHOTO COLLECTION

Welcome to

Sun City Center

"The Town Too Busy To Retire"

GROUPING OF PHOTOS

1. Aerial Views Sun City Center
2. Arts and Crafts
3. Dancing & Exercises
4. Lakes
5. Social Events & Parties
6. Ms Senior Sun City Center
7. Tillers & Toilers
8. Paul Finnegan
9. Golf Carts
10. That's Entertainment
11. Music & Singing
12. Churches
13. Golf Courses
14. Recreation & Leisure
15. Sports Activities
16. United Community College
17. Computer
18. Volunteer Services
19. Nature's Splendor
20. Health Amenities

Aerial Views
Sun City Center

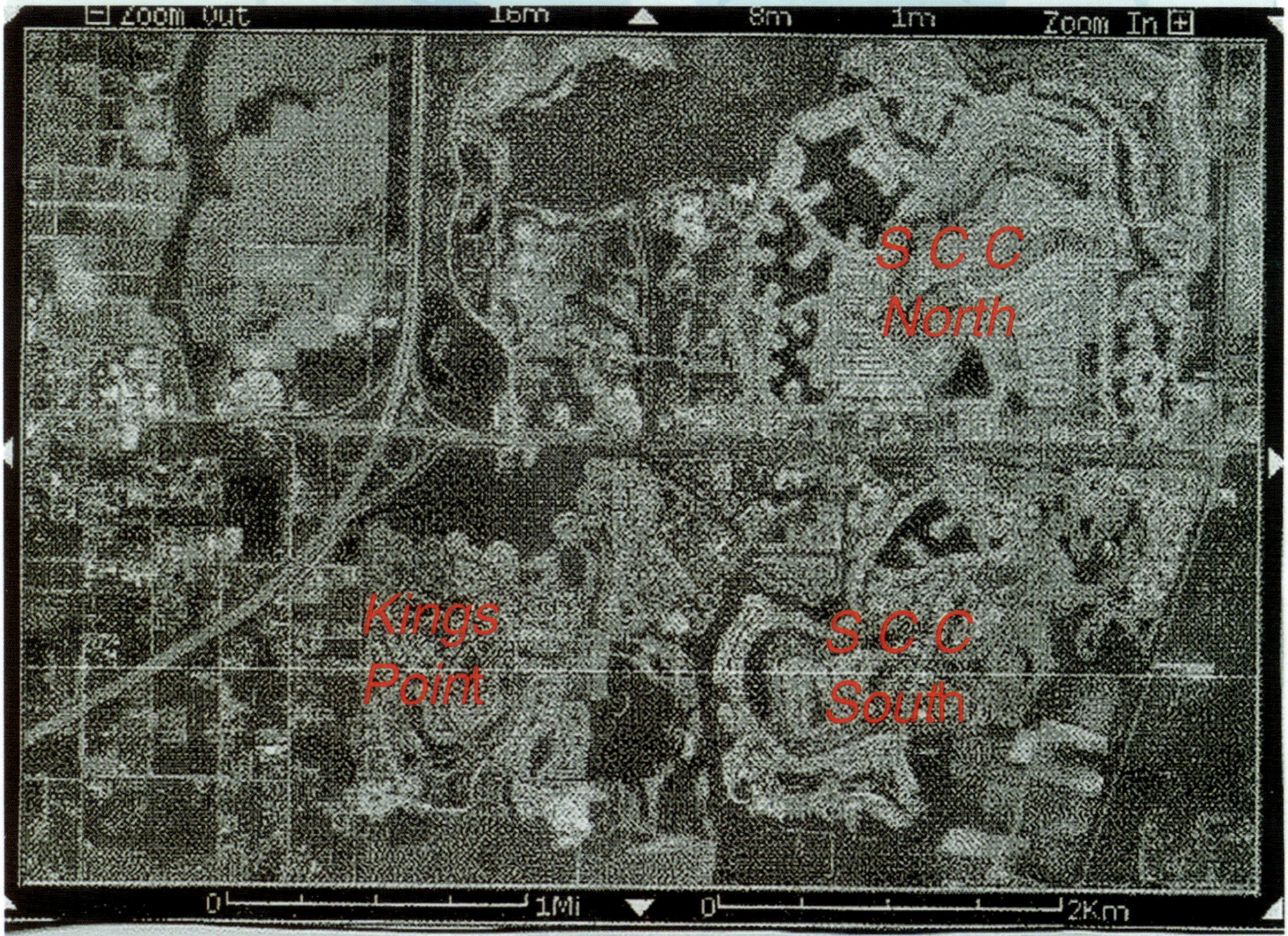

Aerial Photo
Sun City Center

Simmons Lake
New Bedford, S.Pebble Beach,
Flamingo Lane ,
At lower right corner is
Golf & Racquet Club

Aerial Photo
Sun City Center

North Lakes Golf Course
North Pebble Beach Blvd.
Cherry Hills Drive
United Community Church

S

Aerial Photo
Sun City Center

Swan Lake, CA Office, Library, Security Patrol, Recreational complex, North Pebble Beach

E

Aerial Photo
Sun City Center

Lake Towers, Courtyards, Winn Dixie (Market Place)., Sun City Center Plaza, Banks, & Post Office

N

Aerial Photo
Sun City Center

North, Middle, South
Lakes Regions
Danbury Drive
Bunker Hill Drive
Del Webb Blvd. W.

Aerial Photo
Kings Point

KP Entrance Gate, Clubhouse (on top), Kings Blvd. Looking North

N

Aerial Photo Kings Point

KP Gloucester Blvd.
Glendower Circle
Glenmore Circle
Cypress Greens Golf

S

Aerial Photo
Sun City Center

Acacia Lakes Region
Communication Tower
U.S. 301 & E. Del Webb
El Rancho Drive

N

Arts and Crafts

Arts
Pottery
Ceramics
Lapidary
Needle Crafts

China Painting
Photo
Stained Glass
Wood Carving
Saw Dust Engineers

Flower Arranging
Weavers
Sew N Sews
Shellcrafters
Bunka

Art Club

Pottery

Ceramics

THE FALL INTERNATIONAL
Florida Ceramic Show
October 1998
Orlando

Lapidary

Needle Craft

Stained Glass

China Painting

Weavers

Sew N Sews

Shell Crafters

Flower Arrangers

Garden Club

SUN CITY CENTER PHOTO CLUB

Wood Carving

BUNKA

Sawdust Engineers

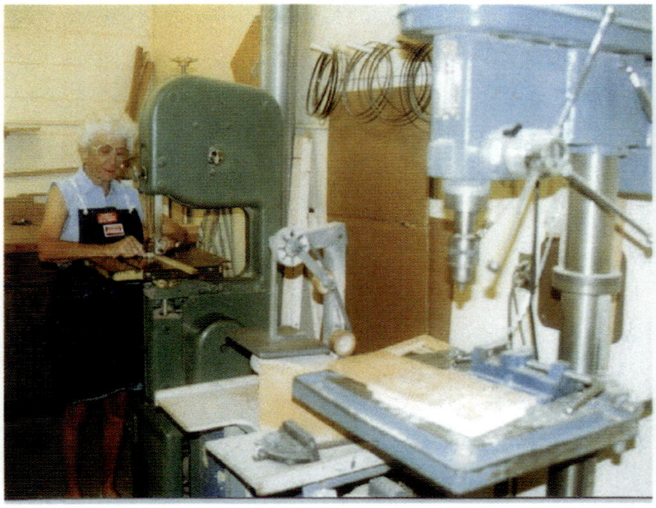

Dancing & Exercises

Ball Room Dance
Square Dance
Round Dance
Tap Dance
Water Dance
Body Language
Dance
Hawaiian Dance

Solo Dance
Clogging

Yoga
Stretch Exercises
Water Exercises
Tai-Chi

Ballroom Dance

SQUARE DANCE

Round Dance

Tap Dancers

Synchronized Swimming

Body Language Dancing

HAWAIIAN DANCING

Solo Dance

Stretch EXercise

Tai Chi

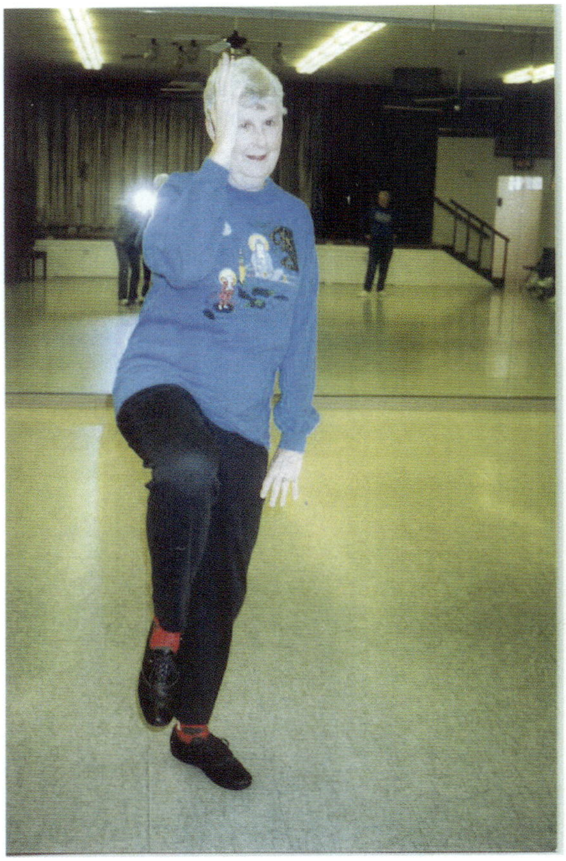

Yoga

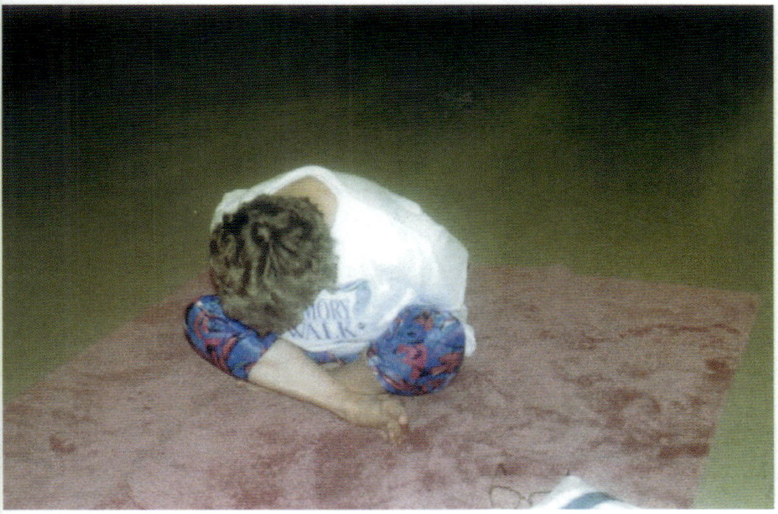

Meditation

Stand on his head

Lakes

North Lake
Middle Lake
South Lake
Swan Lake
Simmons Lake
Wedgewood Lake

North Lake

Middle Lake

Simmons Lake

Swan Lake

South Lake

Social Events & Parties

Good Samaritan Ball
"Hi, Neighbor!"
Memorial Day
July Fourth
Veterans Day
Information Fair
FunFest

Luau Parties
Men's Club Gala
Golf & Racquet Club

Halloween
Christmas Time
New Year's Party

Good Samaritan Ball

Good Samaritan Ball

Hi, Neighbor!

July Fourth

Veterans' Day

Guest Speaker
Paul W. Bucha former Capt., 101st Airborne Division.
President, Congressional Medal of Honor Society

Veterans' Day

Paul W. Bucha with his mother Mrs. Mary Bucha Who is a resident of Kings Point

Information Fair
Oct. 9-10, 1998

Information Fair

A Special Event

Memorial Day

Memorial Day Picnic

Men's Club Gala
Dinner Dance, Auctions & Golf Cart Raffle

Dinner Dance

"Ballerino"

Live Auction

Men's Club Gala

Silent Auctions

Raffles

Portrait

LUAU

LUAU

Halloween

THE SHEET FAMILY
BULL SHEET
3 SHEETS TO THE WIND
FULL OF SHEET

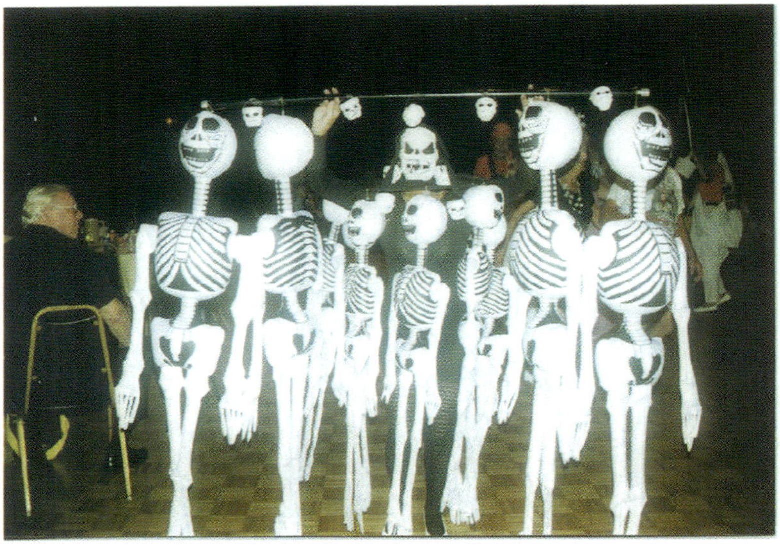

SHEET FAMILY
DONT GIVE SHE!

Christmas Time

Golf & Racquet Club

Happy New Year 1999

Presenting

Ms. Senior Sun City Center

Age of Elegance

The first Ms. Senior
Sun City Center
Ms. Leora Trevino

Age of Elegance

Ms. Sr. Sun City Center Pageant 1998.

Most Talented

TILLERS & TOILERS
Gentleman & Lady Farmers
Living Off The Land

Good Earth

Growing Flowers

Paul Finnegan

A Living Legend
103 Years Young
World War 1 Veteran
Attributes his Longevity to
1. Clean Living
2. Water Exercises

Centennial

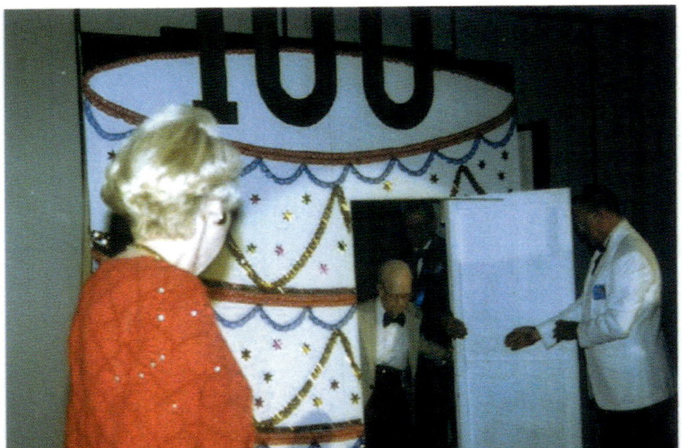

**Golf Carts

A Means of Transportation In Sun City Center

Golf Carts–Go Places

Golf Cart

Annual Inspection

That's Entertainment

SCC Follies

Pelican Players

Entertainers

Half Tone Band

SCC Follies

SCC Follies

Entertainers

KP Half Tone Band
At Florida State Fair

Pelican Players

Pelican Players

Music & Singing

Men's Chorus
Kings Point Chorus
Women's Chorus
Church Choirs

Big Band
Sunday Afternoon
Sing-A-long
Organ Club
Jazz Club

SCC MEN'S CHORUS '99

4 G's Barbershop Quartet

Kings Point Chorus

One Hundred Mixed Voices

Sopranos- Altos -Tenors-Basses

Women's Chorus

Sun City Center Big Band

Our Very Own

Sing-A-Long

Sunday Afternoon

Organ Club

Bob Ralston ***(above)***
in concert in Sun City Center
a famed organist from
Lawrence Welk TV shows

The Jazz Club

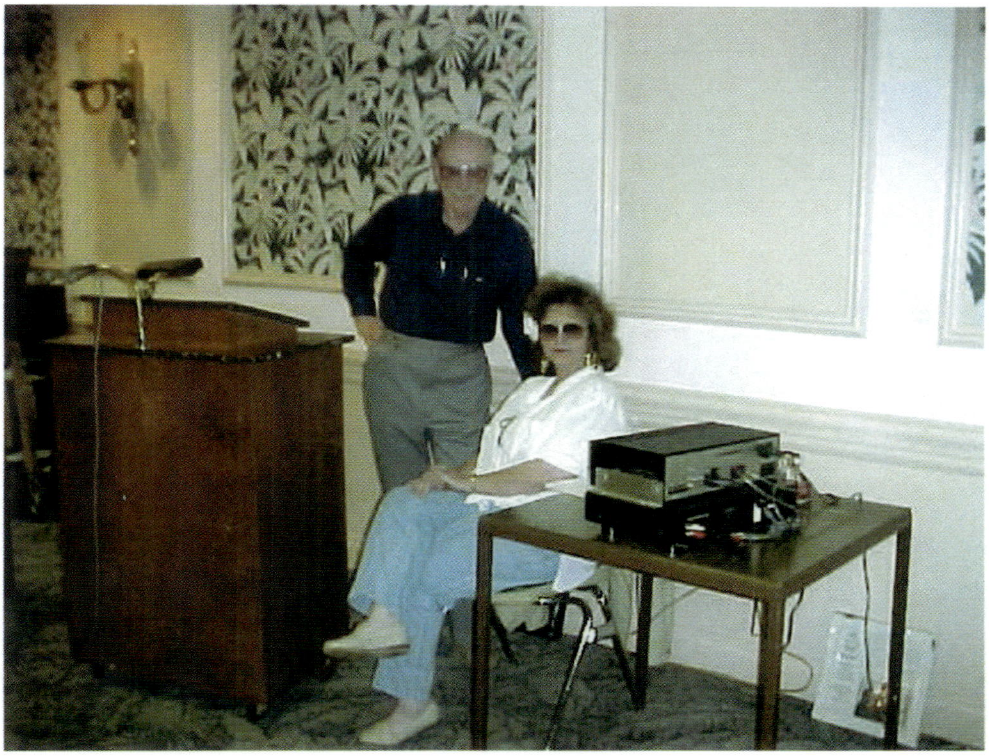

Prince of Peace Catholic Church
United Community Church
Redeemer Lutheran
United Methodist
Trinity Baptist

St. Andrew Presbyterian
Jewish Congregation of
Sun City Center
St. John The Divine Episcopal

Interfaith Social Action Council

Places of Worship

Prince of Peace Catholic Church

United Community Church

Places of Worship

United Methodist Church

St. John The Divine Episcopal Church

Places of Worship

Trinity Baptist Church

Jewish Congregation of Sun City Center

Places of Worship

St. Andrew Presbyterian Church

Redeemer Lutheran Church

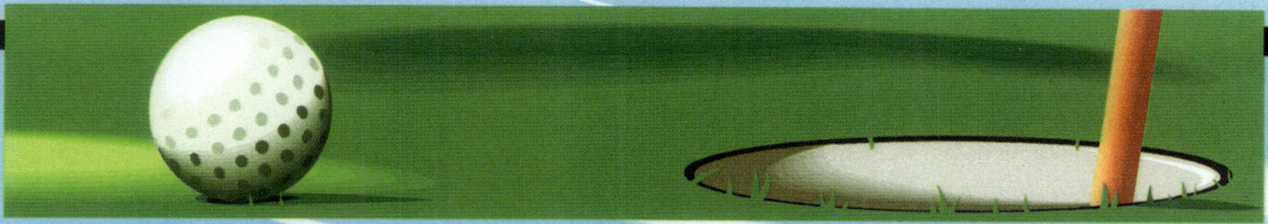

Golf Courses

North Lakes Course
South Course
Caloosa
Caloosa Greens
Cypress Greens

Kings Point Executive

North Lakes Golf Course

South Golf Course

Caloosa Country Club

Caloosa Golf Course
(Private)

Cypress Greens Golf Course

Golf Courses

Caloosa Greens golf

KP Executive golf

Recreation & Leisure
Bridge
Chess
Mah Jongg
Bingo
Billiards
Boating
Fishing
Bicycling
Radio Controlled
Sail Boats
Model Trains
Ham Radio

Games

Bridge

Mah Jongg

Chess

Bingo

Billiards

Bicycling

Sailing on the Bay

Boating

Sailing on Simmons Lake

On Cockroach Bay

On Little Manatee

Fishing

Radio Controlled Sailboats

Model Trains

Ham Radio

Sports Activities
TENNIS
VOLLEY BALL
LAWN BOWLING
SHUFFLE BOARD
SOFT BALL
HORSE SHOES
TABLE TENNIS
SWIMMIING

Tennis

Volley Ball

Lawn Bowling

Shuffleboard

SCC SOFTBALL TEAM

Horse Shoes

Table Tennis

Swimming

United Community College

The United Community College was established in 1976 by the United Community Church of Sun City Center as a continuing education outreach program to serve the entire community and surrounding area. The purpose of the College Program is to inform, to refresh and to inspire.

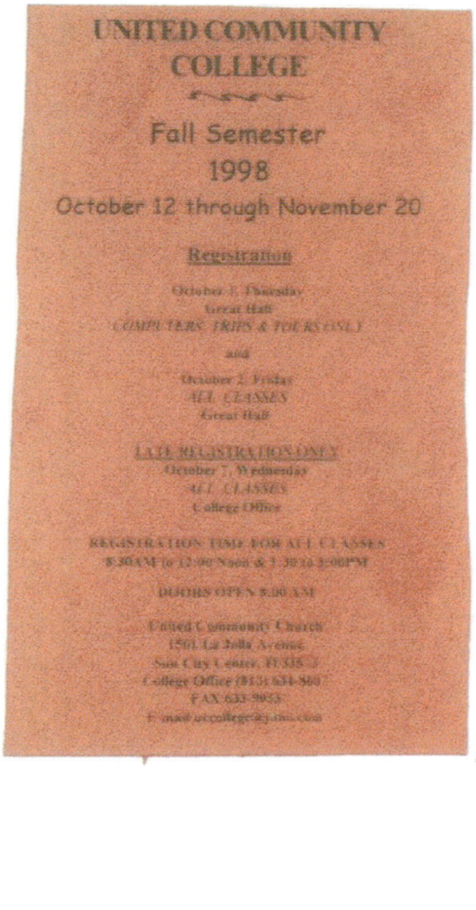

UNITED COMMUNITY
COLLEGE

Fall Semester
1998
October 12 through November 20

Registration

October 1, Thursday
Great Hall
COMPUTERS, TRIPS & TOURS ONLY

and

October 2, Friday
ALL CLASSES
Great Hall

LATE REGISTRATION ONLY
October 7, Wednesday
ALL CLASSES
College Office

REGISTRATION TIME FOR ALL CLASSES
8:30AM to 12:00 Noon & 1:30 to [illegible]PM

DOORS OPEN [illegible] AM

United Community Church
1501 La Jolla Avenue
Sun City Center, FL [illegible]
College Office (813) [illegible]
FAX 633-[illegible]
E-mail [illegible]

Co-Deans

Sally Hahn **Yvonne Ponsor**

Well attended classes

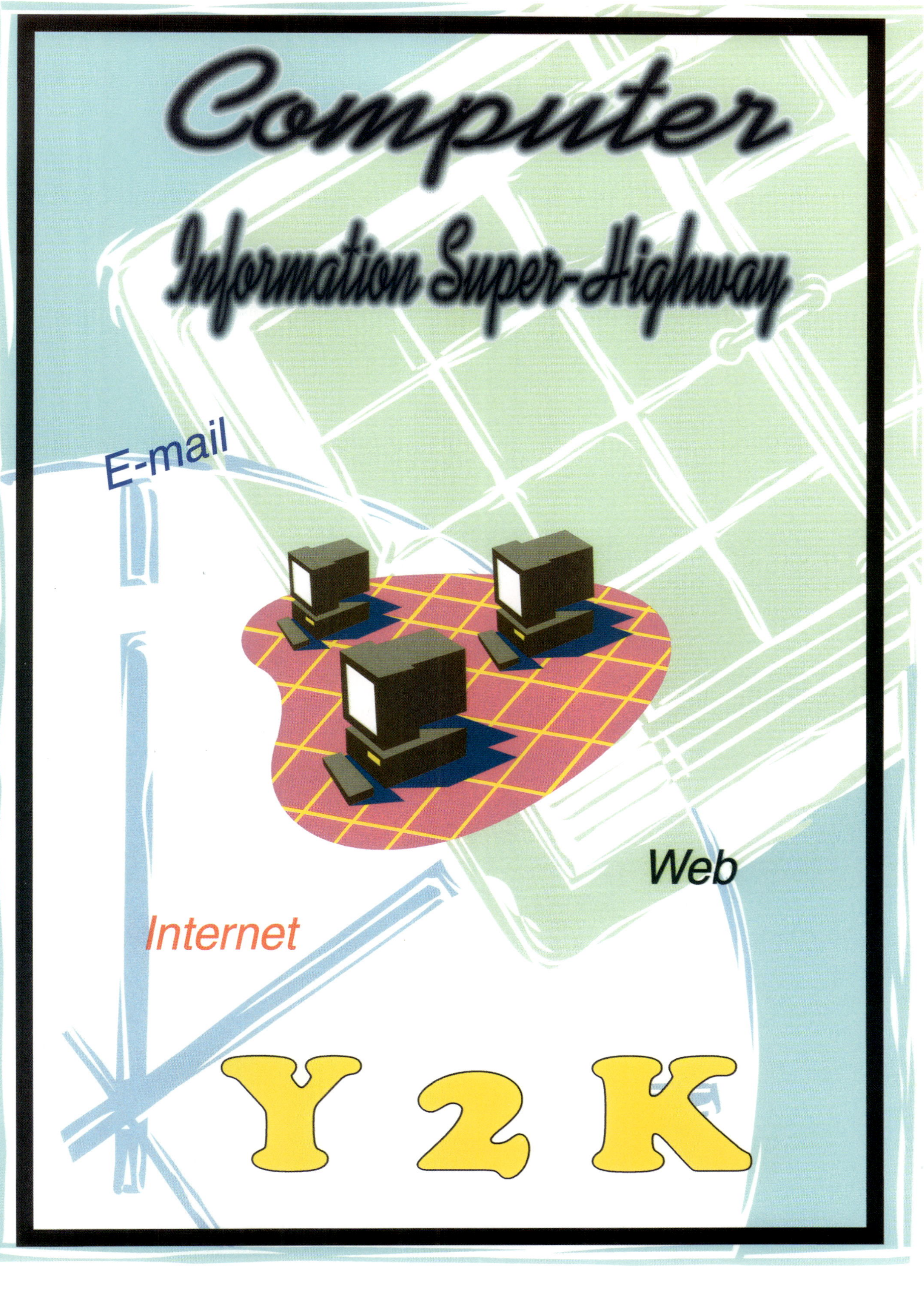
Computer
Information Super-Highway
E-mail
Web
Internet
Y2K

Computer Club

Computer Club

Computer Classes

Volunteer Services
Samaritan Services
Emergency Squad
Security Patrol
SCC Library
Men's Club
Lifeline Program
Meals on Wheels
SCC Woman's Club
Community Foundation of
Greater Sun City Center

Samaritan Services

LENDING
A HELPING
HAND

SAMARITAN SERVICES

An All-Volunteer
Neighbor Assistance Program
For The Greater
Sun City Center Community

Good Samaritan Services

LENDING A HELPING HAND

An All-Volunteer
Neighbor Assistance Program
For The Greater
Sun City Center Community

* Companion Care

* Temporary Transportation

* Sponsoring an Alzheimer Support Group

* Coordinating the Meals-On-Wheels Program

*Operating Adult Day Care Center with Hillsborough County

* Operating a Drop-in Center in Sun City Center

* Sponsoring a Bereavement Support Group

*Provide space in the Samaritan Office for the Bay Area Legal Services

SCC Emergency Squad

The Building

Expeditors

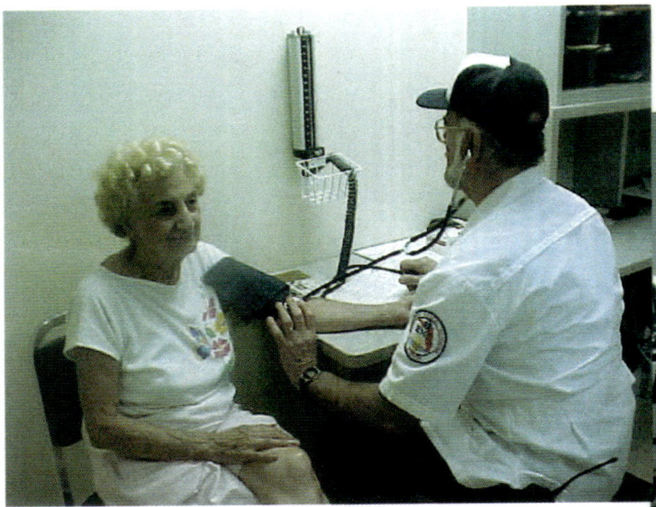

Blood Pressure

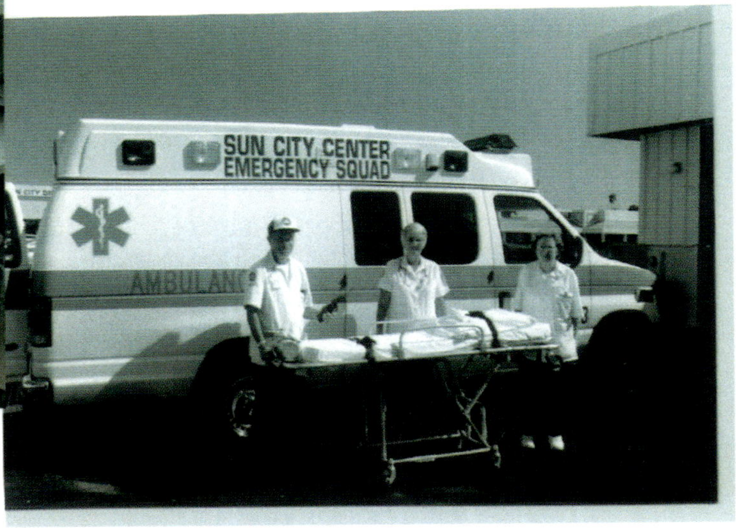

Ambulance

SCC Emergency Squad

The Chief

SCC Security Patrol

The Chief

1995-2001

Dispatcher

Security Patrol & Sheriff Offices

Patrol Cars

Meals on Wheels

SCC Library

Librarian

SCC Library

Community Foundation of Greater Sun City Center

Council Members

"The Foundation enables you to make a permanent contribution back to your community."

A Generous Gift

Samaritan Services, Emergency Squad, Security Patrol, and Library, as beneficiaries, each received a check from the income of a $1 million Endowment Fund established by Janet and Durward Siville through Community Foundation of Greater Sun City Center.

Men's Club
Lifeline Project

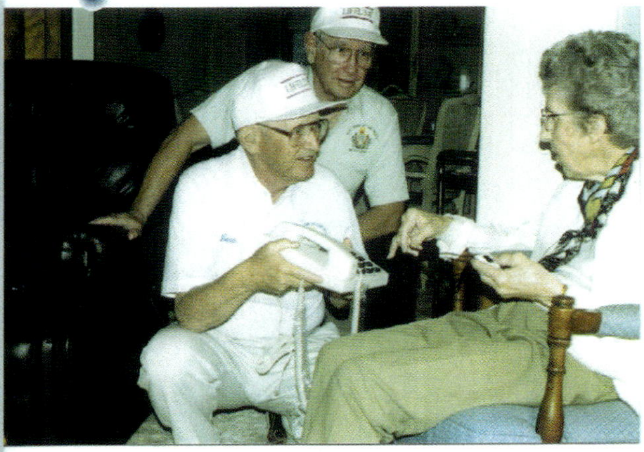

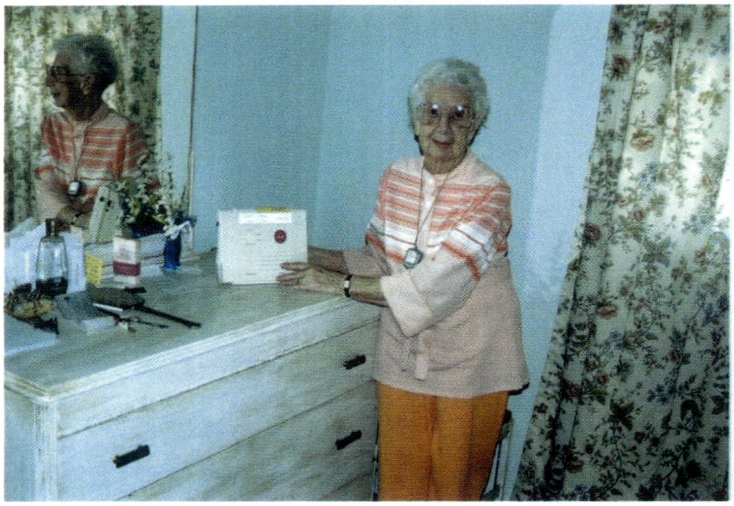

Services to Community also include:
The Open Door Program (Automatic doors for handicapped)
Man to Man Prostate support program

Scholarship Awards Luncheon

SCC WC (Woman's Club)

Nature's Splendor

Clouds & Sky
Sunrise, Sunset
Storm Gathering
Feathered Friends

Nature's Display

Nature's Display

Nature's Display

Storm Gathering

Feathered Friends

Golf Course Visitors

Health Amenities

Swimming Pools
Fitness Center
Indoor Walking Track

Swimming Pools

Indoor Lap Pool

Indoor Walking Pool

Jacuzzi

Outdoor Pool

Fitness Center

Indoor Walking Track